# THE CHRONICLES OF
# KING
# CONAN
## VOLUME ONE

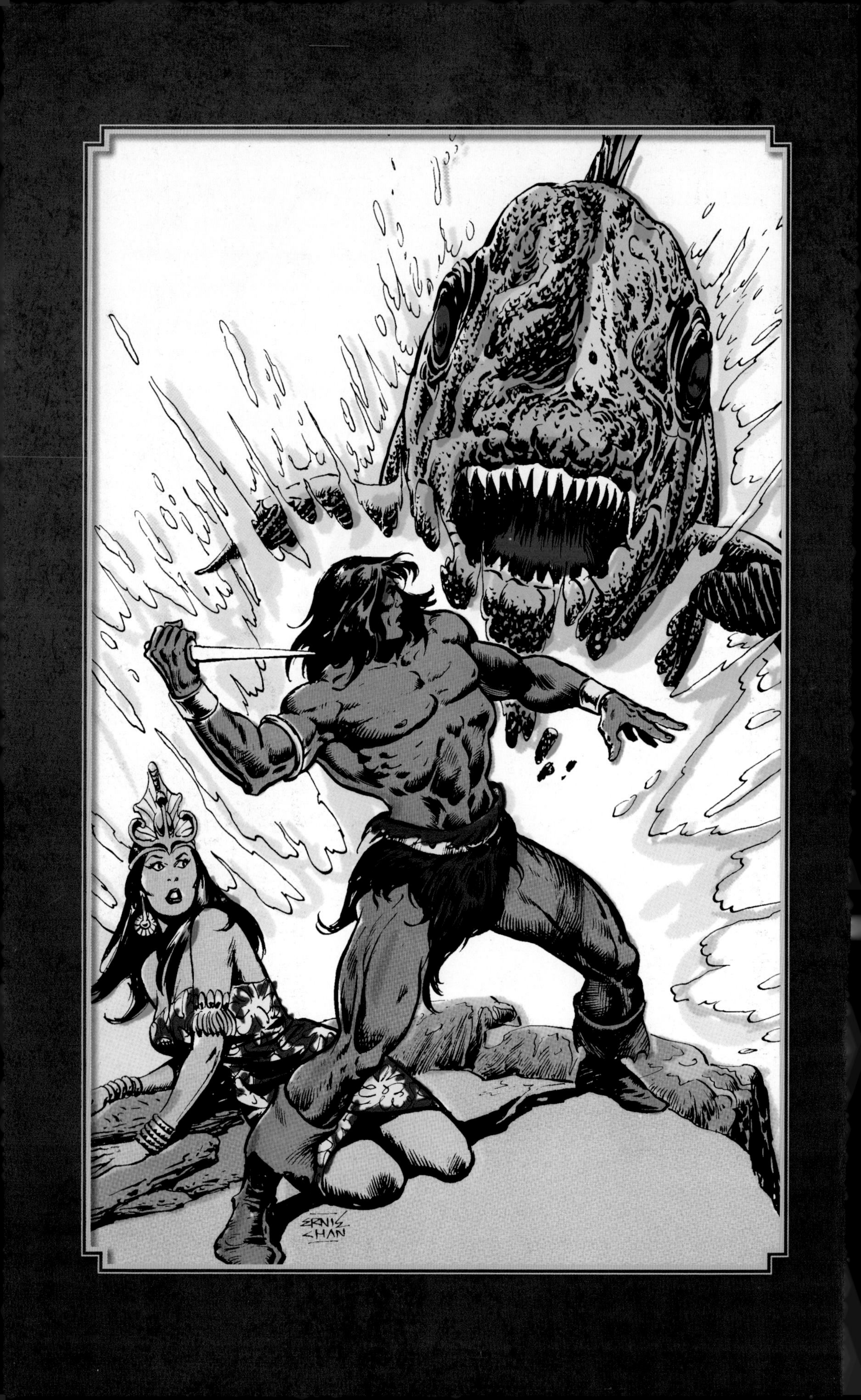
ERNIE CHAN

# THE CHRONICLES OF
# KING
# CONAN
## VOLUME ONE

## THE WITCH OF THE MISTS
### AND OTHER STORIES

Based on the classic pulp character
**Conan the Barbarian**, created by
## ROBERT E. HOWARD

Written by
## ROY THOMAS

Illustrated by
## JOHN BUSCEMA, ERNIE CHAN,
## and DANNY BULANADI

Colored by
## GEORGE ROUSSOS

Lettered by
## JOE ROSEN

OKS®

Publisher
## MIKE RICHARDSON

Assistant Editor
## PATRICK THORPE

Associate Editor
## KATIE MOODY

Editor
## DAVE LAND

Special thanks to Fredrik Malmberg, Joakim Zetterberg,
and Leslie Buhler at Conan Properties.

This volume collects issues #1 through #5
of the Marvel comic-book series *King Conan*.

Published by Dark Horse Books
A division of Dark Horse Comics, Inc.
10956 SE Main Street
Milwaukie, OR 97222

darkhorse.com | conan.com

To find a comics shop in your area, call the Comic Shop Locator Service
toll-free at 1-888-266-4226

First edition: September 2010
ISBN 978-1-59307-477-7

1 3 5 7 9 10 8 6 4 2

Printed at Midas Printing International, Ltd., Huizhou, China

MIKE RICHARDSON President and Publisher   NEIL HANKERSON Executive Vice
President   TOM WEDDLE Chief Financial Officer   RANDY STRADLEY Vice President
of Publishing   MICHAEL MARTENS Vice President of Business Development   ANITA
NELSON Vice President of Marketing, Sales, and Licensing   DAVID SCROGGY Vice
President of Product Development   DALE LAFOUNTAIN Vice President of Information
Technology   DARLENE VOGEL Director of Purchasing   KEN LIZZI General Counsel   DAVEY
ESTRADA Editorial Director   SCOTT ALLIE Senior Managing Editor   CHRIS WARNER
Senior Books Editor   DIANA SCHUTZ Executive Editor   CARY GRAZZINI Director of
Design and Production   LIA RIBACCHI Art Director   CARA NIECE Director of Scheduling

# TABLE OF CONTENTS

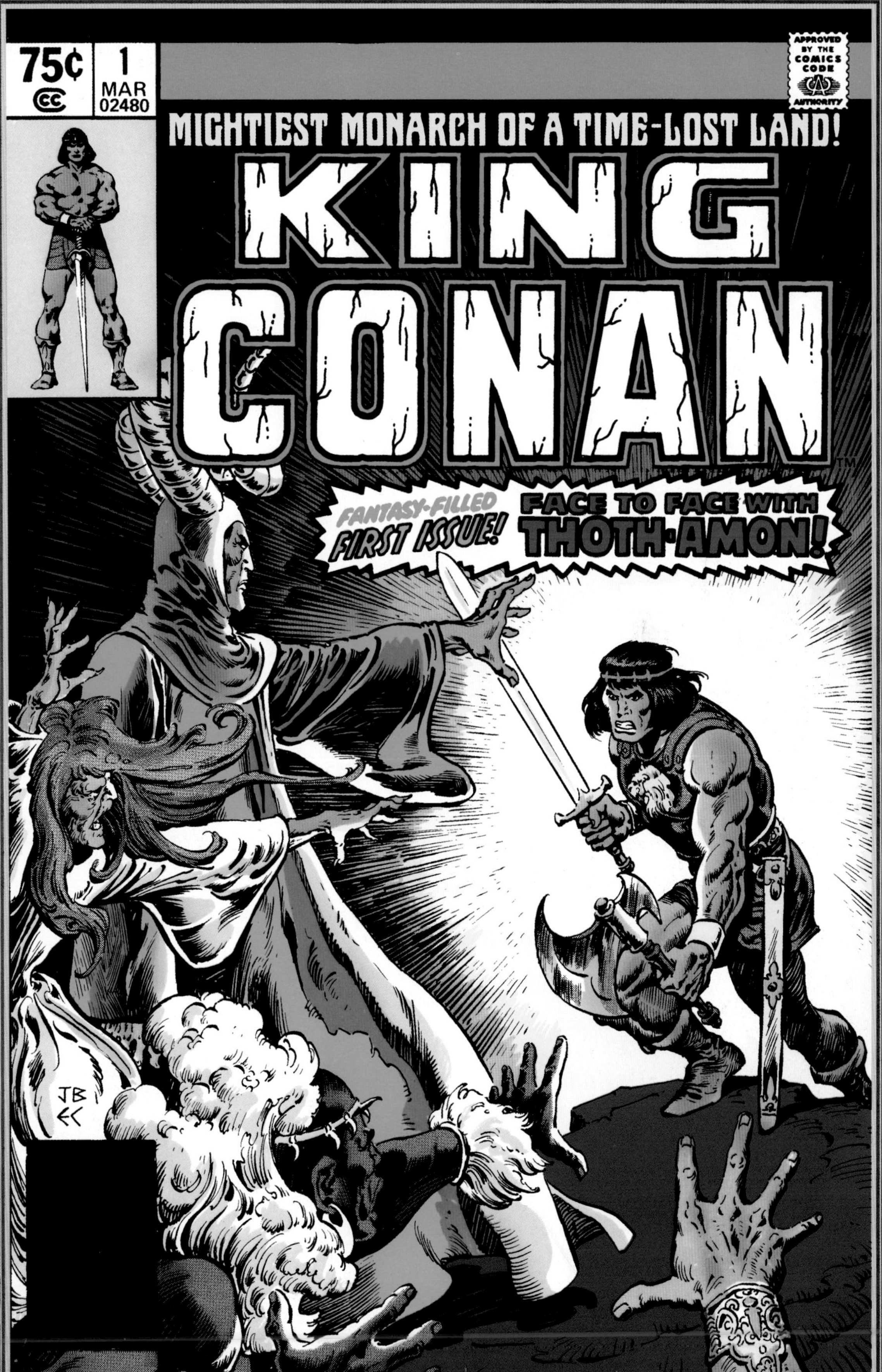
75¢
CC
1
MAR
02480
APPROVED BY THE COMICS CODE AUTHORITY
MIGHTIEST MONARCH OF A TIME-LOST LAND!
KING CONAN
TM
FANTASY-FILLED FIRST ISSUE!
FACE TO FACE WITH THOTH-AMON!
JB EC

THE FIRST AND GREATEST SWORD-AND-SORCERY HERO!

# KING CONAN

FEATURING THE EPIC ADVENTURER CREATED BY ROBERT E. HOWARD

A NEW SERIES OF SWASH-
BUCKLING SORCEROUS SAGAS BY

**ROY THOMAS** & **JOHN BUSCEMA**
WRITER/EDITOR         ILLUSTRATOR

**ERNIE CHAN**, EMBELLISHER

G. ROUSSOS
COLORIST

JOE ROSEN
LETTERER

**JIM SHOOTER**
CONSULTING
EDITOR

LF-379

"KNOW, O PRINCE, THAT THE MAN CALLED CONAN WAS *ALL THINGS* IN HIS DAY, AFTER HE HAD WANDERED SOUTH FROM THE SNOW-CAPPED HILLS OF HIS NATIVE CIMMERIA:

"FIRST A *THIEF*, WITH MORE COURAGE THAN SKILL...THEN A *SOLDIER OF FORTUNE* IN MORE NATIONS AND WITH MORE ARMIES THAN MOST MEN CAN COUNT...

"...AYE, EVEN A *PIRATE* MORE THAN ONCE, FIRST WITH THE SHE-CORSAIR BÊLIT, LATER WITH BOTH THE BLOODY BARACHANS AND THE BUCCANEERS OF ZINGARA.

"THEN, IN HIS *FIFTH DECADE* HE SLEW A VICIOUS TYRANT AND BECAME *KING IN AQUILONIA*, PROUD-EST KINGDOM OF THE VIOLENT HYBOR-IAN AGE.

"IN TIME, HE TOOK A *WIFE:* THE FAIR *ZENOBIA,* AS GENTLE OF SPEECH AS HE WAS SWIFT OF SWORD, YET POSSESSED OF AN INNER WILL OF IRON."

"THE ELDEST OF HIS CHILDREN WAS A *SON,* LIKEWISE NAMED CONAN... BUT MORE USUALLY KNOWN BY HIS SOBRIQUET OF *CONN.*"

"ALL THE WESTERN WORLD DID DO THEM HOMAGE... FOR NOW, AT LAST, THE LION OF AQUILONIA HAD A *CUB... AN HEIR.*"

"AND IT WAS WHEN YOUNG CONN HAD SEEN SOME *TWELVE SUMMERS* THAT THE BROODING, DARKSOME *EVIL* CAME WAFTING FROM BOTH NORTH AND SOUTH... TO BLOW LIKE A *NOXIOUS WIND* ACROSS THE FACE OF THE LAND...."

# The WITCH OF THE MISTS

ADAPTED FROM THE STORY BY **L. SPRAGUE DE CAMP** AND **LIN CARTER**
FEATURING THE HERO CREATED BY **ROBERT E. HOWARD**

THE SUN, HIDDEN BY THE HEAVY OVERCAST, IS NEARING THE WESTERN HORIZON WHEN THE RIDER ON THE GRAY MARE EMERGES FROM THE FOREST, TO JOIN *KING CONAN OF AQUILONIA* IN THE MIST-SOAKED CLEARING...

NO SIGN OF THE *YOUNG PRINCE* BACK ALONG THE *TRAIL*, YOUR MAJESTY.

IS IT POSSIBLE THE LAD HAS RIDDEN *AHEAD*, ON THE SCENT OF THE *WHITE STAG* WE ALL SOUGHT?

SHALL I SUMMON THE *REST* OF THE PARTY, SIRE? 'TWERE NOT GOOD TO LET THE HEIR TO THE THRONE BE LOST IN THE FOREST OVERNIGHT, EVEN HERE IN *GUNDERLAND.**

NO, LET MY SON *BE*!

WE COULD *SPREAD OUT*, SOUNDING HORNS....!

WE'LL ACCOUNT THIS PART OF THE LAD'S *EDUCATION*.

*GUNDERLAND= NORTHERN PROVINCE OF AQUILONIA. --ROY.

IF HE'S THE *STUFF OF KINGS*, A SLIGHT WETTING AND A SLEEPLESS NIGHT WILL BE NOTHING TO HIM!

WHY, WHEN *I* WAS HIS AGE, *MANY* WERE THE BLACK NIGHTS I SPENT IN THE CIMMERIAN HILLS, UNDER THE GLITTER OF THE STARS.

LET'S BACK TO *CAMP*. WE'VE LOST THE WHITE STAG--

--BUT WE HAVE THE *BOAR* WE CAUGHT, AND YOUR KING IS *NIGH STARVED*!

IT WILL SERVE HIM RIGHT IF HE'S *BENIGHTED* IN THESE WOODS-- ESPECIALLY IF THE THRICE-DAMNED *RAINS* BEGIN AGAIN!

IT'S *MORE* THAN POSSIBLE, PROSPERO.

THE FOOLISH CUB HAS IN-HERITED MORE THAN HIS SHARE OF HIS SIRE'S *THICKHEADED-NESS.*

THAT NIGHT, WINE LOOSENS THE BARBARIAN-BORN MONARCH'S TONGUE TO AN UNUSUAL DEGREE, AND *BAWDY ANECDOTES* FROM HIS LONG CAREER POUR FORTH...

...SO THEN, NATURALLY, I *DUMPED* THE FAITHLESS WENCH FROM TWO STORIES HIGH INTO A *CESSPOOL.*

MAY *CROM* AND MITRA SKEWER ME WITH *LIGHTNING* IF I DIDN'T!

ALL THE SAME, PROSPERO NOTICES THAT, FROM TIME TO TIME, CONAN *CEASES* HIS FORCIBLY LIGHTHEARTED CAROUSING...

...SILENCING THE OTHERS' LAUGHTER WITH A LIFTED HAND, TO LISTEN FOR DISTANT **HOOFBEATS**...

...OR TO PROVE **THE BLACKNESS** OF THESE GLOOMY FORESTS NORTH OF TANASUL WITH HIS DEEP-SET EYES OF VOLCANIC BLUE.

PROSPERO KNOWS THAT, WHATEVER HIS EARLIER WORDS, CONAN IS FAR MORE **WORRIED** OVER PRINCE CONN'S FAILURE TO RETURN THAN HE WISHES KNOWN.

DOUBTLESS HE FEELS **PANGS OF GUILT,** SINCE THE HUNTING TRIP TO NORTHERN GUNDERLAND WAS HIS OWN IDEA:

HIS QUEEN, ZENOBIA, FELL SERIOUSLY **ILL** AFTER GIVING BIRTH TO THEIR THIRD CHILD, A DAUGHTER.

DURING THE SLOW MONTHS OF HER RECOVERY, CONAN HAS BEEN **WITH** HER AS MUCH OF THE TIME AS HE CAN AFFORD TO TAKE FROM HIS ROYAL DUTIES.

FEELING **NEGLECTED,** AS BOYS OF TWELVE ARE WONT TO DO, YOUNG CONN BECAME SURLY AND WITHDRAWN...

THUS, NOW THAT ZENOBIA HAS REGAINED MUCH OF HER STRENGTH, AND DEATH'S DARK WINGS SEEM **FAR** FROM THE PALACE ONCE MORE...

...THE KING SUGGESTED A FEW WEEKS OF **CAMP-ING** AND **HUNTING,** HOPING TO FIND A NEW **CLOSENESS** TO HIS SON AND HEIR-APPARENT.

AND NOW IT SEEMS THE HEADSTRONG LAD, WILD WITH THE EXCITEMENT OF HIS FIRST GROWN-UP HUNT, HAS RIDDEN OFF ALONE INTO AN **UNKNOWN FOREST**...

...IN MAD PURSUIT OF THE ELUSIVE **SNOW-WHITE STAG** WHICH THEY ALL CHASED IN VAIN FOR LONG HOURS.

THEN, ABRUPTLY, THE SKY *CLEARS*... AND, BREAKING OFF IN THE MIDST OF A RAMBLING TALE OF HIS BUCCANEER DAYS, THE KING *SNARLS*...

--BUT I'LL SIT HERE *NO LONGER!*

WITH THIS BRIGHT MOON, I CAN FOLLOW A TRAIL OR I'M A *STYGIAN.*

SADDLE UP *RED YMIR* FOR ME; THE BLACK'S *WINDED.*

CALL ME *WOMAN-HEARTED* IF YOU DARE, MAY CROM CURSE MY BONES--

SIR *VALENS!* DISTRIBUTE THE TORCHES, AND LET'S *FORTH!*

I'LL NOT SLEEP TONIGHT TILL I KNOW MY *BOY* IS SAFE!

THOSE WHO JOURNEY WITH THE KING ARE NO *FOOLS:* THEY HAVE EXPECTED THIS OUTBURST FOR SOME TIME NOW.

NOR WOULD ANY *OBJECT,* EVEN IF HE COULD-- FOR PRINCE CONN IS MUCH BELOVED AMONG BOTH NOBLES AND SERVANTS OF KING CONAN'S COURT...

BUT, ALL KNOW THAT THERE BE *OTHER* MEN -- ROGUES, THIEVES, AND RENEGADES, WHO OFTEN TAKE TO THE WILDS -- AYE, NOT TO MENTION GREAT *BEARS* AND GRAY *WOLVES* HERE IN GUNDERLAND.

WHEN I FIND THAT UNLICKED CUB, I'LL BEAT HIS *PANTS* FOR PULLING US FROM A WARM FIRE!

JUST THEN, A SNOW-WHITE *OWL*-- AN OMEN OF SORTS-- FLOATS ACROSS THE MOON'S FULL FACE.

HOO HOO HOO

WHAT THE *DEVIL*--?

AND, EVEN AS HE RIDES, CONAN RECALLS HIS OWN PEOPLE'S WHISPERED TALES OF A *WHITE WERE-STAG,* SWIFT AS THE WINTER WIND.

PRAY CROM IT'S *NOT* SUCH A DEMON-THING HIS *FIRSTBORN SON* HAS PURSUED INTO THE NIGHT-SHROUDED FOREST.

PRINCE CONN IS COLD, WET, WEARY... AND *LOST*.

ALWAYS, THE *WHITE STAG* HAS FLOATED AHEAD OF HIM, LIKE A GHOSTLY *BIRD*, GLIMMERING AGAINST THE DARKNESS... BUT AT THIS MOMENT, HE DOES NOT SEE *IT* ANY MORE THAN HE SEES A *TRAIL BACK*.

HE *DOES* KNOW, HOWEVER, THAT HE'LL BE RECEIVING A DESERVED *HIDING* FROM HIS *SIRE* WHEN HE DOES RETURN...

...UNLESS, PERHAPS, HE RIDES BACK *TRIUMPHANT*, TO THROW THE GREAT STAG AT THE *FEET* OF THE KING.

IT IS THAT THOUGHT WHICH ALLOWS YOUNG CONN TO SHRUG OFF HIS *FATIGUE* AND HUNGER... AND TO *RIDE ON*.

THEN, AS HIS *BLACK PONY* SHOULDERS THROUGH THE WET, DRIPPING BOUGHS INTO A LONG GRASSY *GLADE*-- HE BEHOLDS *IT* ONCE AGAIN:

THE WHITE STAG!

UP, MARDUK!

IRON-SHOD HOOVES DRUM THROUGH THE SWISHING, WET BLACKNESS... AS THE BOY'S HEART *SWELLS*, THE EXCITEMENT OF THE HUNT MAKING HIS BLOOD SING.

AND EVER *AHEAD* OF HIM, LIKE A WILL-O'-THE-WISP, THE WHITE STAG *GLOWS*.

BUT THEN, A DENSE WALL OF *TREES* RISES BEYOND... AND CONN KNOWS THE STAG MUST *SLOW* ITS PACE OR ELSE GO FLOUNDERING INTO THAT BARRIER.

A FEW MOMENTS MORE, AND THE LITHE PRINCE FLINGS BACK ONE ARM TO HURL HIS *JAVELIN*...

*HAH!* THERE'S NOWHERE FOR YOU TO *GO*, IS THERE, GHOST-STAG?

I CAN'T WAIT TO SEE THE *LOOK* ON MY FATHER'S FACE WHEN I--

*CROM AND MITRA!*

EVEN THE LAD'S STRICT *SIRE* AND WATCHFUL *MOTHER* WOULD DOUBTLESS FORGIVE HIM FOR THE OATH THAT NOW ESCAPES HIS LIPS--

--AS, NOT THIRTY FEET DISTANT FROM HIM, THE STAG SUDDENLY *DISSOLVES INTO MIST*--

--A MIST THAT INSTANTLY *REFORMS* ITSELF--

--INTO A TALL, GAUNT *HUMAN* SHAPE--

--A *WOMAN*, CLOTHED IN ROBES AS THE STAG'S HIDE HAD BEEN--

--A WOMAN WITH A BILLOWING CLOUD OF *IRON-GREY HAIR*--

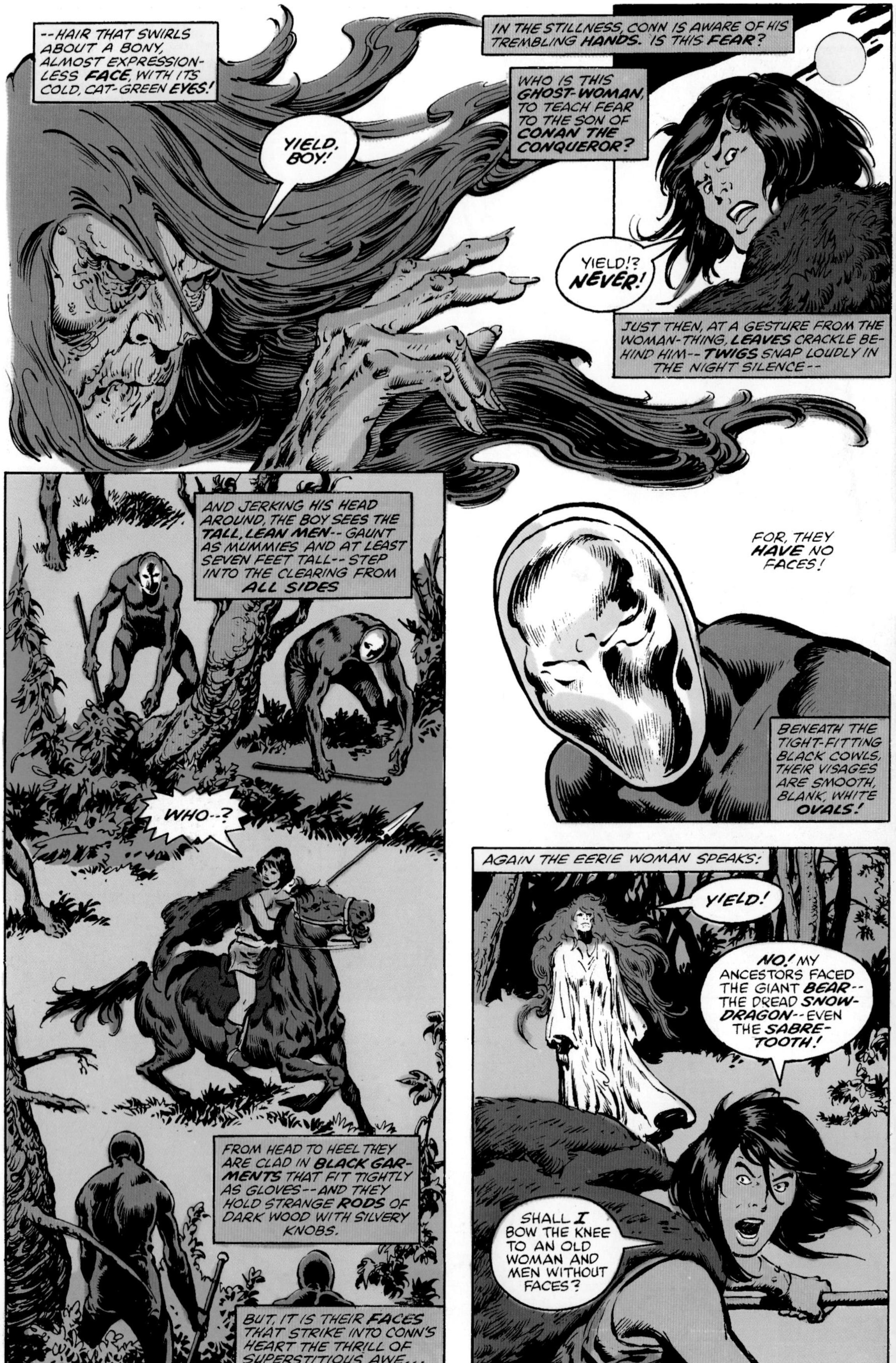
--HAIR THAT SWIRLS ABOUT A BONY, ALMOST EXPRESSION-LESS FACE, WITH ITS COLD, CAT-GREEN EYES!
YIELD, BOY!
IN THE STILLNESS, CONN IS AWARE OF HIS TREMBLING HANDS. IS THIS FEAR?
WHO IS THIS GHOST-WOMAN, TO TEACH FEAR TO THE SON OF CONAN THE CONQUEROR?
YIELD!? NEVER!
JUST THEN, AT A GESTURE FROM THE WOMAN-THING, LEAVES CRACKLE BE-HIND HIM--TWIGS SNAP LOUDLY IN THE NIGHT SILENCE--
AND JERKING HIS HEAD AROUND, THE BOY SEES THE TALL, LEAN MEN--GAUNT AS MUMMIES AND AT LEAST SEVEN FEET TALL--STEP INTO THE CLEARING FROM ALL SIDES
WHO--?
FROM HEAD TO HEEL THEY ARE CLAD IN BLACK GAR-MENTS THAT FIT TIGHTLY AS GLOVES--AND THEY HOLD STRANGE RODS OF DARK WOOD WITH SILVERY KNOBS.
BUT, IT IS THEIR FACES THAT STRIKE INTO CONN'S HEART THE THRILL OF SUPERSTITIOUS AWE...
FOR, THEY HAVE NO FACES!
BENEATH THE TIGHT-FITTING BLACK COWLS, THEIR VISAGES ARE SMOOTH, BLANK, WHITE OVALS!
AGAIN THE EERIE WOMAN SPEAKS:
YIELD!
NO! MY ANCESTORS FACED THE GIANT BEAR--THE DREAD SNOW-DRAGON--EVEN THE SABRE-TOOTH!
SHALL I BOW THE KNEE TO AN OLD WOMAN AND MEN WITHOUT FACES?

THEN, YELLING THE **CIMMERIAN WAR-CRY** LEARNED FROM HIS MIGHTY **SIRE**, THE YOUTH **CHARGES** THE SINISTER, SURROUNDING FIGURES--

YET, BEFORE HIS PONY CAN MAKE MORE THAN ONE WEARY **BOUND**--

YEEEE-AHH!

OWWW

--RAISING HIS **JAVELIN**, TO HURL IT AT THE NEAREST OF THE FACELESS ONES!

--AGONIZING **PAIN** SHOOTS UP HIS ARM, AND HIS WEAPON DROPS FROM **NUMB** FINGERS!

STILL, WITH AN INARTICULATE CRY, CONN CATCHES WITH HIS REMAINING HAND AT THE **SWORD** THAT CLINGS TO HIS HIP--

--EVEN AS, WITH MAGICAL SWIFTNESS, ONE OF THE BLACK-CLAD MEN GRASPS HIS MOUNT'S **BRIDLE** WITH A BONY HAND!

YOU THINK IT'S *THAT* EASY, DO YOU?

WELL, WE SHALL *SEE!*

WITH A GURGLING **GROAN**, THE TALL MAN FOLDS AT THE KNEES AND FALLS FACE-DOWN IN THE WET GRASS...

*REAR,* MARDUK! *REAR!*

BUT, LIKE PHANTOMS, HIS ATTACKERS *EVADE* THOSE IRON-SHOD HOOVES...

AND THEN-- THE SILVERY **KNOB** OF ONE OF THE HAND-HELD RODS STRIKES THE BOY'S **WRIST**--

≥UNNH--!≤

--AND HIS SWORD **FLIES** FROM FLACCID FINGERS.

**ANOTHER** METAL BALL GENTLY STROKES THE BACK OF HIS **HEAD**--

OHHHH

--AND HE **FALLS** FROM THE SADDLE, A BUNDLE OF LOOSE LIMBS.

AH, SO WE **HAVE** HIM--!

**CONN**-- CROWN PRINCE OF AQUILONIA-- HEIR APPARENT TO THE THRONE OF **KING CONAN!**

**THOTH-AMON** WILL BE **PLEASED!**

Come Morning:

HO, SIRE!

IT'S **EURIC**-- MY CHIEF HUNTS-MAN!

AYE, MAJESTY-- WE SENT HIM ON **AHEAD.**

WHAT HAVE YOU *FOUND*, EURIC?

*THIS*, SIRE...!

AN *IVORY MASK*-- FEATURELESS, EXCEPT FOR THE EYE SLITS.

*HYPERBOREAN* WORK, CURSE THAT LAND OF DEVILS!

ANYTHING... *ELSE?*

*BLOOD* ON THE GRASS-- THE GRASS IT-SELF TRAMPLED-- *HOOFMARKS* OF A YOUNG PONY--

--AND-- *THIS*, I FEAR--!

THE *FALCHION* I GAVE CONN-- ON HIS LAST *BIRTHDAY!*

AND WAS THERE-- NOTHING *MORE?*

WHEN THEY'VE FOUND THE TRACK, SOUND YOUR *HORN* AND GATHER THE MEN!

THE *DOGS* ARE SNIFFING ABOUT FOR A TRAIL *NOW*, SIRE.

ONCE AGAIN, THE KING OF AQUILONIA *SHIVERS*...AS IF AN UNSEEN DRAFT OF *ICY AIR* WERE BLOWING UPON HIS HEART.

THE SUN IS AN HOUR OLDER WHEN THEY FIND THE *CORPSE*, BURIED BENEATH A MOUND OF DEAD LEAVES...

SOMETIME *LAST NIGHT*, SIRE.

HE'S BEEN *STRIPPED* OF ANY CLOTHES HE MIGHT HAVE WORN-- BUT *MITRA!* HE WAS NIGH *SEVEN FEET TALL!*

HE WAS A *HYPERBOREAN*, ALL RIGHT...

NO OTHER MEN ON EARTH HAVE SUCH A BUILD ALONG WITH THAT *PALE SKIN*-- THE SILKY, COLORLESS HAIR--

--AND NOW, THOSE DEAD, CAT-GREEN *EYES!*

SOON, THE HOUNDS LOOSED AGAIN, THE PARTY RIDES ON TOGETHER, BENEATH AN OVERCAST SKY...

WE'RE BEING *LED*, PROSPERO.

YOU THINK THE MASK AND FALCHION WERE LEFT BEHIND FOR A *PURPOSE*, SIRE?

I *KNOW* THEY WERE-- IN MY *BONES*, THE WAY AN OLD STIFF-LEGGED SOLDIER KNOWS WHEN RAIN IS COMING.

THERE'S A *PACK* OF THOSE WHITE DEMONS AHEAD SOMEWHERE.

THEY HAVE MY *BOY*-- AND THEY'RE *HERDING* US, DAMN THEIR HIDES!

INTO AN *AMBUSH*, PERHAPS?

I DOUBT IT. WE'VE RIDDEN SAFELY THROUGH *THREE* PERFECT SITES FOR SUCH A TRAP IN THE LAST HOUR.

NO, THEY'VE SOME *OTHER* PURPOSE IN MIND.

MAYBE THEY'RE HOLDING THE YOUNG PRINCE FOR *RANSOM!?*

OR FOR *BAIT!*

I WAS A *CAPTIVE* IN HYPERBOREA ONCE-- AND WHAT I SUFFERED AT THEIR HANDS GAVE ME NO CAUSE TO *LOVE* THOSE BONY VULTURES--

NOR HAS WHAT I *DID* THERE, ERE I TOOK MY LEAVE OF THEIR HOSPITALITY, GIVEN THEM REASON TO LOVE *ME!*

WHAT MEANS THE *IVORY MASK?*

IT'S A SHADOWY *LAND OF DEVILS*-- CLOAKED EVER IN CLAMMY *MISTS*, AND RULED BY NAKED, GRINNING *FEAR...*

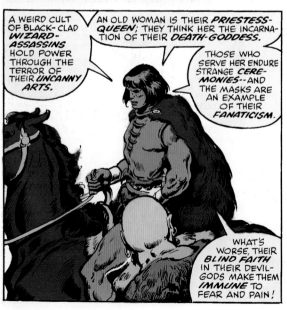

A WEIRD CULT OF BLACK-CLAD *WIZARD-ASSASSINS* HOLD POWER THROUGH THE TERROR OF THEIR *UNCANNY ARTS.*

AN OLD WOMAN IS THEIR *PRIESTESS-QUEEN*; THEY THINK HER THE INCARNATION OF THEIR *DEATH-GODDESS.*

THOSE WHO SERVE HER ENDURE STRANGE *CERE-MONIES*-- AND THE MASKS ARE AN EXAMPLE OF THEIR *FANATICISM.*

WHAT'S WORSE, THEIR *BLIND FAITH* IN THEIR DEVIL-GODS MAKE THEM *IMMUNE* TO FEAR AND PAIN!

THEY RIDE FORWARD WITHOUT FURTHER WORDS.

THEN, TOWARDS *EARLY AFTERNOON*, NEAR THE PLACE WHERE MEET THE FRONTIERS OF AQUILONIA, CIMMERIA, NEMEDIA, AND THE BORDER KINGDOM...

*HOLD!* LOOK YOU THERE!

THAT'S CONN'S *JAVELIN*, OR I'M A *PICT!*

AYE, SIRE-- BUT THERE'S A ROLL OF *WHITE PARCHMENT* TIED TO IT--!

AS I'D *EXPECTED!* BRING IT HERE, EURIC!

THE MESSAGE IS CRUDELY SCRAWLED IN AQUILONIAN...

THE KING SHALL GO FORWARD ALONE TO *POHIOLA.* IF HE DOES THIS, THE SON OF HIS LOINS WILL NOT BE HARMED. IF HE DOES OTHER THAN THIS, THE CHILD WILL DIE IN WAYS IT IS NOT WHOLESOME TO DESCRIBE. THE KING SHALL FOLLOW THE PATH MARKED WITH THE *WHITE HAND.*

...AND IT IS WRITTEN... IN *BLOOD.*

CONAN SITS HIS HORSE, BROODING DARKLY BENEATH THE GLOOMY SKY, AS PROSPERO READS THE PARCHMENT TO THE MEN.

"...MARKED WITH THE *WHITE HAND.*"

BUT SURELY, SIRE, YOU'LL *NOT* GO!

WITHOUT *US* WITH YOU, YOU'LL STAND *NO CHANCE* AGAINST--

I RIDE TO FIND MY *SON,* HUNTS- MAN.

PROSPERO, HERE IS MY GOLDEN *SEAL- RING;* IT WILL MAKE YOU *REGENT* OF MY KINGDOM UNTIL I RETURN... OR UNTIL MY INFANT *SECOND* SON GROWS UP, IF I DON'T COME BACK.

I SUPPOSE THERE'S *NO* USE TRYING TO--

THERE ISN'T.

THEN GO WITH ... , CONAN OF AQUILONIA--

--BUT, BY THE GODS, I'LL GATHER AN *ARMY* AT TANASUL AND RIDE AFTER YOU, TO *INVADE* HYPER- BOREA ON YOUR HEELS-- AND MAKE FOR THE *CITADEL OF POHIOLA!*

DO WHAT YOU *WILL!*

BY THEN, I'LL EITHER HAVE *FREED* CONN-- OR ELSE JOINED HIM IN *DEATH!*

MOUNTED NOW ON BARON GUILAIME'S **BIG GRAY**, TO REPLACE HIS OWN WINDED ROAN, CONAN RIDES FORWARD THROUGH THE LAND CALLED THE **BORDER KINGDOM**...

...A DREARY **WASTE** OF DESOLATE, EMPTY MOORS AND COLD, UNEASY WINDS.

AT FIRST HE CAN FOLLOW THE **TRACKS** LEFT BY THE HYPERBOREANS IN THE MUDDY SOIL, AND HE PUSHES HIS STALLION HARD...

FOR, THERE IS THE SLIMMEST OF CHANCES THAT HE MIGHT **CATCH UP** WITH THE PALE-SKINNED DEVELOPS BEFORE THEY REACH THEIR FORTRESS.

SOON, THE TRAIL **FADES OUT** ON THE STONY SOIL... BUT THERE STILL IS LITTLE CHANCE TO **LOSE** THE TRAIL...

FOR, NOW AND AGAIN, HE PASSES A **SIGN** THAT HIS SON'S ABDUCTORS HAVE LEFT BOTH TO TAUNT AND TO GUIDE HIM:

THE IMPRINT OF A **HAND**, WHITE AGAINST SOIL OR EVEN SOLID ROCK!

WITCHCRAFT!

HOUR AFTER HOUR HE RIDES STEADILY ON, STRIVING NOT TO REMEMBER THAT HIS OFFSPRING IS *CAPTIVE* OF THE WITCHMEN... AS THE WORLD DARKENS TOWARD *NIGHT*.

ONE BY ONE THE FEW *STARS* COME OUT, THOUGH A *HAZE* OVERHANGS MOST OF THE SKY.

TOWARD *DAWN*, HE CAN RIDE NO MORE... BUT BUILDS A SMALL FIRE WITH DRY BRACKEN, AND FALLS INTO A HEAVY *SLEEP*.

FOR *THREE DAYS* HE RIDES EVER DEEPER INTO THIS DESOLATE WASTELAND, SKIRTING THE *SWAMP BORDERS* OF THE GREAT SALT MARSH.

ON THE THIRD DAY, *TWILIGHT* COMES, PLUNGING THE TREACHEROUS BOGLAND IN *GLOOM*...

...WHEN, AT A *FORKING* OF THE PATH:

*SO!* THEY DON'T WANT TO TAKE A CHANCE I'D *LOSE MY WAY*, EH?

THEY DON'T EVEN *MIND* THAT I KNOW I'M GALLOPING STRAIGHT INTO A *TRAP*.

THE MOON'S COLD FACE IS MASKED BEHIND A LACY VEIL OF VAPOR, AS HE DRIVES HIS STALLION ALONG THE PATHWAY MARKED BY THE *WHITE HAND*.

THEN, SUDDENLY, *AMID* THE THICKENING DARKNESS--

--THE MUDDY HEATHER IS *ALIVE* WITH MEN!

BY THE BONES OF *CROM!*

THESE ARE *BEASTMEN*-- FILTHY, GAUNT, NAKED SAVE FOR TWISTS OF GREASY RAG ABOUT THEIR LOINS-- *SNARLING* AS THEY ADVANCE UPON HIM!

ROARING A DEEP-CHESTED *CHALLENGE*, CONAN MAKES HIS STAND--!

YOU HAIRY DOGS RULE THE *SWAMP COUNTRY*, AYE--

--BUT *I* RULE BY THE STRENGTH OF MY *SWORD-ARM!*

*LEGEND* WHISPERS THAT THE BEASTMEN ARE THE DEGENERATE SPAWN OF GENERATIONS OF ESCAPED *CRIMINALS* AND RUNAWAY *SLAVES* WHO FLED HITHER FOR SANCTUARY.

CENTURIES OF *INBREEDING*-- OF LIVING OUTSIDE OTHER HUMAN CONTACT-- HAS DEBASED THEM TO LITTLE ABOVE THE LEVEL OF *ANIMALS.*

NOW, THEY *SWARM* OVER HIM, EVEN AS HALF A DOZEN OF THEM DIE IN THE BLOOD-SPATTERED MARSH--

--TILL BOTH *MAN* AND *MOUNT* ARE DRAGGED DOWN BY THE SHEER *WEIGHT OF NUMBERS*--

GRARRR

-- AND CONAN'S WORLD *EXPLODES!*

*UNNNH!*

While:

OUT OF THE DIM AND SWIRLING *MISTS* THE RUDE CASTLE RISES-- A MIGHTY KEEP BUILT OF HUGE, CYCLOPEAN BLOCKS OF UNMORTARED STONE, GHASTLY IN THE DIM STARLIGHT.

WORN AND WEARY FROM DAYS AND NIGHTS OF TRAVEL, PRINCE CONN BLINKS *BLEARY EYES* AT IT.

AS THEY DRAW CLOSER AND HE SEES ITS GREAT PORTCULLIS LIFTING, THE HALF-STARVED BOY REPRESSES A *SHUDDER*...FOR THE RISE OF THE SPIKED GRILL OF RUSTY IRON IS LIKE THE SLOW YAWN OF A GIGANTIC *MONSTER*.

BUT HE IS *CONN, SON OF CONAN*...SO HE SAYS NOTHING.

THROUGH THE VAST *PORTAL* THEY RIDE AND STALK, INTO AN ENORMOUS HALL WEIRDLY LIT WITH THE FLICKERING LIGHTS OF TORCHES.

THE PORTCULLIS COMES DOWN BEHIND THEM, TO RING AGAINST THE STONE PAVE LIKE THE *KNELL OF DOOM.*

COLD WHITE HANDS PLUCK THE BOY FROM THE SADDLE, TO TOSS HIM INTO A CORNER, AMID FILTH-STREWN STRAW.

OBSERVANT EVEN NOW, AMID THE GLOOM, HE SEES THAT THE WHOLE CASTLE IS ONE *TREMENDOUS HALL*, WITH ITS ROOF-RAFTERS LOST IN *DARKNESS* HIGH ABOVE.

THEN, AT A MUTTERED COMMAND FROM THE OLD WOMAN...

YOU'RE-- CUTTING MY *BONDS!?*

BUT *WHY*--?

OH, *I* SEE!

YOU DON'T WANT ME TO *STARVE* WHILE YOU FIGURE OUT MY *RANSOM*, IS THAT IT?

BUT, AS THE YOUTH DEVOURS THE COLD, TASTELESS SCRAPS, HE KNOWS SOMEHOW THAT THERE WILL *BE* NO RANSOM...

...THAT HE IS MEANT *NEVER* TO LEAVE THIS VAST HALL... *ALIVE.*

HIS **FATHER** HAS TAUGHT HIM, HOWEVER, TO **ACCEPT** WHAT YOU CANNOT CHANGE...

THE DULL SOUND OF A **GONG** AWAKENS HIM... AND CONN FINDS THAT, IN THIS GLOOMY PILE OF STONE WHERE THE **LIGHT OF DAY** NEVER PIERCES, HE HAS **LOST** ALL SENSE OF TIME.

THE SMALL GONG, HE SEES, IS CARVED IN THE SHAPE OF A **HUMAN SKULL.**

...AND CATCH SUCH **SLEEP** AS WILL REFRESH YOU, IN CASE YOU **CAN** CHANGE IT, AFTER ALL!

AND, ON A CIRCULAR STONE DAIS IN THE HALL'S CENTER, THE **WITCHWOMAN** IS SEATED, AS A GREAT COPPER BOWL OF GLOWING COALS SHEDS A WAVERING LIGHT THE COLOR OF **BLOOD** ON HER FACE.

THEN, THE **WITCHMEN** ENTER, STILL CLAD IN THEIR COWLS AND MASKS... BUT NOT **ALONE.**

CONN RECALLS THAT IN THE **SWAMP** DAYS BEFORE, THEY HAD TAKEN THIS MAN **CAPTIVE.**

-- AS HE PLAYS UNWILLING WITNESS TO A **TERRIBLE** CEREMONY--

NN NGAA! NNGGAAA!!

≥NNGGHH--!?≤

DESPITE THE POOR DEVIL'S NIGH-BESTIAL STATE, CONN FEELS A SUDDEN **PITY** FOR THIS WRITHING, HELPLESS, PLEADING SPECIMEN--

--AND THE VICTIM SLOWLY GOES LIMP.

ALL THIS TIME, THE AGED PRIESTESS HAS STARED SIGHTLESSLY AHEAD... SWAYING FROM SIDE TO SIDE, HUMMING A TUNELESS AIR...

...AS, AMID THE THIN, EERIE MOAN OF HER SONG, PUNCTUATED BY THE MONOTONOUS RHYTHM OF THE GONG, THE SMOKE GROWS, FED BY CRIMSON WINE.

AS FOR CONN: HE STARES WITH HELP-LESS FASCINATION... AS THE SMOKE BEGINS TO EDDY TO AND FRO, AS IF TO THE TOUCH OF INVISIBLE HANDS, MOLDING IT... SHAPING IT.

FOR, THE ROILING CLOUD OF SMOKE IS TAKING THE SHAPE OF A MAN...TALL,GAUNT...DRAPED IN EASTERN ROBES.

AND SUDDENLY, CONN KNOWS HE HAS HEARD THOSE ALOOF, AQUILINE FEATURES DESCRIBED IN GRIM DETAIL...BY HIS FATHER!

HAIL, O LOUHI...!

GREETINGS... THOTH-AMON!

NOW, IN TRUTH, DO THE CHILLY CLAWS OF FEAR CLOSE AROUND CONN'S HEART...FOR HE KNOWS HE IS IN THE CLUTCHES OF EARTH'S MIGHTIEST EVIL MAGICIAN...

CROM.

...THE STYGIAN SORCERER WHO HAS SWORN, LONG SINCE, TO BRING CONAN THE CIMMER-IAN DOWN TO A TERRIBLE DEATH--AND TO CRUSH AQUI-LONIA ITSELF INTO THE MIRE!

IT IS *NEAR SUNRISE* WHEN CONAN STRUGGLES GROGGILY BACK TOWARD CONSCIOUSNESS...

≥UNNNHH--!≤

*THE BEAST-MEN--!*

HIS HEAD ACHES ABOMINABLY, AND THERE IS DRIED BLOOD ON HIS SCALP-- BUT HE *STILL LIVES!*

HIS QUASI-HUMAN ATTACKERS, IT SEEM HAVE BORNE THEIR *DEAD* AND THEIR *LOOT* OFF INTO THE NIGHT...

...LEAVING HIM NAKED BUT FOR BOOTS AND LOIN-CLOTH.

FOR A MOMENT, HE WONDERS THAT THEY DID NOT MAKE CERTAIN *HE* WAS DEAD...

THEN, SEARED INTO A NEARBY LOG, HE SEES WHAT *DROVE* THE BEAST-MEN AWAY:

THE *WHITE HAND!*

THERE IS NAUGHT ELSE TO DO BUT GO ON *AFOOT,* A RUDE CUDGEL IN HIS HAND.

IT HAS BEEN *MANY YEARS* SINCE THIS KING OF PROUD AQUILONIA WAS LAST FORCED TO *HUNT AND KILL* TO LIVE...

...AND HE IS *GLAD* THE OLD SKILLS DIE HARD.

HE DEVOURS THE MARSH-BIRD PLUCKED BUT *RAW*...

...DEFENDING HIS CATCH FROM THE WILD *SWAMP-DOGS* THAT WOULD TAKE IT FROM HIM.

AND EVER, HE KEEPS MOVING *NORTH* AND *EAST.*

THE BORDER BETWEEN THE BORDER KINGDOM AND *HYPERBOREA* IS MARKED BY A CURIOUS MONUMENT CALCULATED TO STRIKE *FEAR* INTO THE HEARTS OF MEN:

FOR, WHERE THE TRAIL WINDS THROUGH A NARROW PASS BETWEEN TWO LOW HILLS, THERE LIES A *SKULL*--MAN-LIKE IN SHAPE, BUT MANY TIMES *LARGER* THAN THAT OF A MAN, AND SHINING GRAY-WHITE THROUGH THE GLOOM AND DAMP.

BUT AS CONAN STUDIES THE VAST, NAKED DOME, A *GRIM SMILE* TUGS AT HIS LIPS.

FOR, HE HAS TRAVELED *FAR* IN HIS YEARS OF ADVENTURING... AND HE RECOGNIZES THE GRISLY RELIC AS THE SKULL OF A *MAMMOTH*, ITS TELLTALE TUSKS LONG SINCE SAWN AWAY.

SPITTING, CONAN FEELS HEARTENED.

THOSE WHO USE *TRICKERY* TO INSPIRE SUPERSTITIOUS FEAR ARE OBVIOUSLY FAR FROM *INVULNERABLE.*

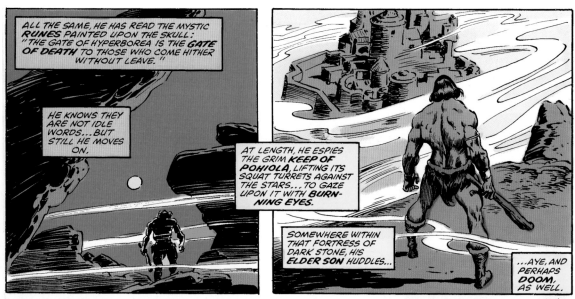

ALL THE SAME, HE HAS READ THE MYSTIC *RUNES* PAINTED UPON THE SKULL: "THE GATE OF HYPERBOREA IS THE *GATE OF DEATH* TO THOSE WHO COME HITHER WITHOUT LEAVE."

HE KNOWS THEY ARE NOT IDLE WORDS...BUT STILL HE MOVES ON.

AT LENGTH, HE ESPIES THE GRIM *KEEP OF POHIOLA*, LIFTING ITS SQUAT TURRETS AGAINST THE STARS...TO GAZE UPON IT WITH *BURNING EYES*.

SOMEWHERE WITHIN THAT FORTRESS OF DARK STONE, HIS *ELDER SON* HUDDLES...

...AYE, AND PERHAPS *DOOM*, AS WELL.

THE DOOR IS OMINOUSLY *OPEN*-- AND CONAN STRIDES IN, PASSING AT ONCE INTO THE *CENTRAL HALL.*

THERE, HE SEES...THE *OLD WOMAN*, WHOM HE KNOWS CAN ONLY BE *LOUHI*, PRIESTESS-QUEEN OF THE WITCH-MEN.

HIS BOOTHEELS RINGING ON THE STONE PAVE, HE MAKES NO ATTEMPT AT *STEALTH* AS HE DRAWS NEAR HER...

YET, SHE *IGNORES* HIM, OR SEEMS TO, UNTIL HE STOPS, ONLY YARDS FROM HER.

*THOTH-AMON* SAYS I SHOULD *SLAY* YOU ON THE SPOT--

--OR AT THE VERY LEAST LOAD YOU WITH *CHAINS* HEAVY ENOUGH TO BIND *TEN MEN!*

LET ME SEE MY *SON.*

33

LOUHI CONTINUES CALMLY, AS IF HE HAD NOT SPOKEN:

THOTH-AMON SAYS YOU ARE THE MOST *DANGEROUS* MAN IN THE WORLD...BUT I HAVE ALWAYS THOUGHT THAT THOTH-AMON WAS *HIMSELF* MORE DANGEROUS THAN ANY OTHER MAN LIVING.

IT IS *ODD.* ARE YOU REALLY SO DANGEROUS?

I WANT TO SEE MY *SON.*

YOU DO NOT LOOK SO DANGEROUS TO *ME*, THOUGH YOU ARE DOUBTLESS STRONG AND BRAVE, WITH GREAT POWERS OF ENDURANCE.

STILL, YOU ARE ONLY A *MAN.*

I CANNOT UNDER-STAND WHAT THERE COULD BE ABOUT YOU THAT MOVES THOTH-AMON TO *FEAR.*

HE FEARS ME BECAUSE HE KNOWS THAT I AM HIS *DOOM.*

AS I SHALL BE *YOURS*, UNLESS YOU TAKE ME TO MY *SON.*

HER EYES OF LAMBENT GREEN GLARE COLDLY INTO HIS OF SMOLDERING, VOLCANIC BLUE...

HER GAZE INTENSIFIES, COLD AND PIERCING... BUT HIS GLOWER DOES NOT FALTER...

AND IT IS THE *GREEN* EYES THAT FALL AT LAST, AND LOOK AWAY...

TAKE HIM TO HIS SON!

SHE DOES NOT LOOK UP AS THE WITCHMAN ENTERS, AND SOME OF THAT CALM STRENGTH HAS *LEFT* HER RASPING VOICE.

WORDLESSLY, THE GAUNT HYPERBOREAN LEADS THE BRONZED INTRUDER TO A STONE-LINED *PIT*...

...INTO WHOSE DARKNESS CONAN *DESCENDS*, WITH-OUT HESITATION, BY MEANS OF A ROPE.

THE ROPE, OF COURSE, IS *DRAWN UP* WHEN HE REACHES THE BOTTOM.

HE KNOWS IT WILL *NOT* BE LOWERED AGAIN AT HIS COMMAND.

THEN, HIS EYES SWIFTLY BECOMING ACCUSTOMED TO THE DARK, HE SPIES THE *FIGURE* HUDDLED AGAINST ONE WALL OF THE SHAFT...

FATHER--!?

CONN!

SPRINGING TO HIS FEET, THE YOUNGSTER FLINGS HIMSELF INTO HIS SIRE'S POWERFUL ARMS.

AND CONAN, CRUSHING THE BOY TO HIM IN A FIERCE HUG, GROWLS SULFUROUS *CURSES* TO DISGUISE THE TENDERNESS HE FEELS...

FATHER!!

...A TENDERNESS CALLED *UNMANLY* IN HIS GRIM, HARD HOMELAND.

NOR DO OLD HABITS DIE EASILY:

YOU UNGRATEFUL *WHELP!* I'LL MAKE YOUR HIDE AS *TAN* AS MINE IS *BRONZE!*

AND I SHALL *DESERVE* IT, FATHER.

THEN AGAIN-- YOU FOUGHT BRAVELY AND WELL: WE FOUND THE *HYPERBOREAN* YOU SLEW, THOUGH THE DOGS TRIED TO HIDE HIM.

MAYBE I'LL *THINK* ABOUT THAT HIDING... WHEN WE'RE BACK IN *TARANTIA.*

FATHER-- YOUR OLD ENEMY *THOTH-AMON,* OF WHOM YOU'VE OFTEN TOLD ME, IS IN THIS!

I KNOW. WHAT ELSE CAN YOU TELL ME?

WELL...WHEN THOTH-AMON HEARD YOU WERE CROSSING THE BORDER KINGDOM ALONE, HE WANTED HER TO *KILL* YOU WITH HER *MAGIC*... BUT SHE REFUSED.

ANY IDEA *WHY?*

I...I THINK SHE WANTS TO KEEP US BOTH *ALIVE* FOR A WHILE... AS A WAY OF KEEPING THOTH-AMON UNDER HER *CONTROL.*

THEY ARE IN SOME SORT OF *PLOT* TOGETHER-- WITH A LOT OF *OTHER MAGICIANS* ALL OVER THE *WORLD!*

CROM!

THOTH-AMON'S A LOT STRONGER AND MORE IMPORTANT THAN THE OLD WITCH-- BUT AS LONG AS SHE HAS *YOU*, HE DOESN'T DARE TRY TO *BOSS* HER TOO MUCH!

YOU MAY WELL BE RIGHT, BOY. DID YOU OVERHEAR ANYTHING MORE ABOUT THIS-- *PLOT*?

PLOT AGAINST *WHAT*?

AGAINST THE *KINGDOMS OF THE WEST*, FATHER!

THERE'S A SORT OF *WIZARDS' GUILD* IN THE LANDS FROM STYGIA SOUTH, IT SEEMS-- SOMETHING CALLED THE *BLACK RING*--!

I KNOW OF IT; THOTH-AMON USED TO BE ITS *HEAD*.

WELL, EVIDENTLY HE *IS* ITS HIGH CHIEF, NOW--

--AND HE'S TRYING TO LEAGUE *HIS* BUNCH WITH THE *WHITE HAND*-- AND WITH SOMETHING FROM WAY OUT IN THE FAR EAST CALLED THE *SCARLET CIRCLE*!

AT THIS NEWS, CONAN BROODS IN SILENCE.

SOON, WHEN THE WORN-OUT LAD HAS TOLD HIS FATHER ALL HE KNOWS, HE FALLS *ASLEEP*, PILLOWED AGAINST CONAN'S BRAWNY TORSO.

BUT, HIS ARM ABOUT THE SHOULDERS OF HIS SON IN A GENTLY PROTECTIVE EMBRACE, HIS *SIRE* DOES NOT SLEEP.

RATHER, HE STARES GRIMLY INTO THE *DARKNESS*, WONDERING WHAT THE FUTURE WILL BRING...BOTH FOR THEMSELVES, AND FOR THE BRIGHT YOUNG KINGDOMS OF THE WEST.

Some Time Later:

WHILE A THUNDEROUS *STORM* RAGES WILDLY OUTSIDE, THREE MEN AND A WOMAN SIT UNSPEAKING ABOUT A VAST COPPER BOWL FILLED WITH GLOWING COALS.

BETWEEN THEM IS STRETCHED AN OMINOUS *TENSION* IN THE DANK, COLD AIR...

...AS THEY *WATCH* ONE ANOTHER OUT OF THE CORNERS OF THEIR EYES.

THEN, ESCORTED BY A DOUBLE FILE OF THE BLACK-CLAD ONES, *CONAN* AND HIS *SON* ARE BROUGHT TO THE FOOT OF THE DAIS...

...WHERE CONAN STARES DIRECTLY INTO THE ICY, SHADOWED EYES OF *THOTH-AMON OF STYGIA*, WHO SPEAKS TO HIM IN HEAVILY ACCENTED AQUILONIAN:

SO, WE MEET *AGAIN*, DOG OF A CIMMERIAN WHO HAS BECOME A *KING!*

CONAN'S ANSWER IS FAR *BRIEFER*...AND EVEN MORE TO THE *POINT*.

VERY WELL, THEN, IF YOU *WILL* PLAY THE DEFIANT ONE, LET ME INTRODUCE YOU TO THOSE *HOSTS* YOU DO NOT KNOW...

THIS IS THE DIVINE *PRA-EUN*, LORD OF THE *SCARLET CIRCLE*... SACRED GOD-KING OF JUNGLE-GIRDED *ANGKHOR* IN THE REMOTE EAST.

THE SO-GREAT KING OF AQUILONIA AND I ARE *OLD FRIENDS*... THOUGH HE KNOWS ME *NOT*.

HE ONCE DID ME THE KINDEST OF *FAVORS*.

OH? I KNOW NOT THIS TALE, PRA-EUN.

BUT *YES!* JUST OVER A DECADE AGO, HE DID TO DEATH THE FORMIDABLE *YAH CHIENG*, SORCERER OF KHITAI-- MY GREATEST *RIVAL*.

HAD HE NOT SLAIN YAH CHIENG, I SHOULD NOT TODAY BE THE *SUPREME MASTER* OF THE SCARLET CIRCLE.

I AM MOST *BEHOLDEN* TO THE BRAVE MONARCH OF AQUI-LONIA.

BUT THERE IS NO WARMTH IN THE EASTERNER'S VOICE...

...AND THOTH-AMON CONTINUES:

THIS, CIMMERIAN, IS THE GREAT SHAMAN *NENAUNIR*, PROPHET AND HIGH PRIEST OF *DAMBALLAH*-- AS HIS PEOPLE CALL *FATHER SET*-- IN FAR OFF *ZEMBABWEI*.

AT ONE WORD FROM NENAUNIR, *THREE MILLION BLACKS* WILL ARISE-- TO STEEP ALL THE WORLD SOUTH OF KUSH WITH *FLAME AND BLOOD!*

THIS MAN DOES NOT LOOK SO DANGEROUS TO *ME*, THOTH-AMON, WITHOUT THE AQUILONIAN *ARMY* BEHIND HIM!

WHY DO YOU *FEAR* HIM SO, STYGIAN?

A *DARKER HUE* STAINS THE FEATURES OF THOTH-AMON... BUT, BEFORE HE CAN SPEAK--

I *AGREE* WITH THE LORD OF ZEMBABWEI!

THAT IS WHY I HAVE PLANNED A SMALL *ENTERTAINMENT* FOR THE PLEASURE OF MY GUESTS. *KAMOINEN!*

AT LOUHI'S BIDDING, ONE OF THE *WITCHMEN* STEPS FORTH...

YOU HAVE BUT TO *COMMAND*, O AVATAR OF THE WHITE HAND!

BEAT THE CIMMERIAN TO HIS *KNEES* BEFORE US-- SO THAT MY COLLEAGUES CAN SEE THEY HAVE *LITTLE* TO FEAR FROM HIM!

AYE, O QUEEN...!

YOUNG CONN HAS ALREADY TOLD HIM OF THE *POWER* OF THOSE SLIM BLACK RODS, OF COURSE...

YET NOW, SUDDENLY, BURSTING FREE, THE BOY CRIES OUT IN *CIMMERIAN*-- WHICH ONLY HE AND HIS SIRE UNDERSTAND--!

*FATHER!* REMEMBER WHAT I TOLD YOU ABOUT *HOW* THEIR WITCH-RODS WORK!

THEN, THIN STRONG *FINGERS* PULL THE LAD BACK.

CONAN RECALLS WHAT HIS SON TOLD HIM HOURS AGO:

THAT THE WITCHMEN PLY THEIR RODS AGAINST SENSITIVE *NERVE* CLUSTERS!

NOISELESSLY, THE TWO MEN *CIRCLE* EACH OTHER FOR LONG, TENSE MOMENTS...

THEN, AS CONAN SEEMS TO LOWER HIS GUARD FOR AN INSTANT, HIS OPPONENT LEAPS TO THE *BAIT!*

YET, IT SENDS A *BOLT* OF *PAIN* LANCING THROUGH HIS BODY!

AS THE ONCE-BARBARIAN SMASHES HIS FOE WITH AN *IRON FIST,* THE POWER-ROD SCARCELY *GRAZES* HIS LEFT SHOULDER--

ARRF!

≥UNNHH!≤

*HERE, LOUHI!* MY KNEES ARE BENT, RIGHT ENOUGH--

--BUT ONLY SO THAT I MAKE *BETTER USE* OF YOUR PALE-HAIRED, BLOODLESS WORSHIPPER--

--THAN HE HAS EVER SEEN *BEFORE!*

AAAAA A

AS THE FLAILING FIGURE HITS THE HUGE *COPPER BOWL,* IT GOES OVER WITH A NOISY CLANG--

--AND THE *NEXT* SOUND HEARD IN THE VAST HALL IS THE *SCREAMING* OF LOUHI, AS HER WHITE ROBES SUDDENLY *BURST AFLAME!*

AAIIEE E

LOOK OUT, PRA-EUN! THE COALS--!

IN HIS CLUMSY HASTE TO FLEE, HOWEVER, THE SMALLER MAN **KNOCKS OVER** HIS OWN THRONE--

AAAGGG

--TRIPPING ACROSS ITS LEGS, TO FALL **INTO** THE PUDDLE OF FIRE!

NOW, AT LAST, THE **WITCH-MEN** ACT--

UGKK

--BUT THEY ARE **TOO LATE!**

NOR HAS CONAN TUTORED HIS **SON** FOR NAUGHT IN THE ART OF ROUGH-AND-TUMBLE...

UNNH

...USING **ALL** WEAPONS AT HIS DISPOSAL!

UMMFE

AND, IN A SEQUENCE OF TEN SECONDS, HE FELLS **FOUR MEN** WITH A WOODEN STOOL...!

THEN COMES THE WAR-CRY OF **NENAUNIR** --

SHAKA-LA!!!!

A HEAVY WOODEN **THRONE-CHAIR** IS LIFTED AND HURLED BY THE SHAMAN OF ZEMBABWEI--

BUT, CONAN **DODGES** IT WITH A STILL PANTHERISH AGILITY--

--AND IT SMASHES INTO THE CIRCLE OF HIS HYPERBOREAN **FOES**, SENDING THEM SPRAWLING LIKE TENPINS!

ARRRR

**HAH!** WITH YOUR HOSTESS' VILE **MINIONS** OUT OF THE WAY, THOTH-AMON--

--IT'S TIME I SETTLED MY LONG-STANDING SCORE WITH **YOU!**

YET, ALREADY, THE STYGIAN MAGE GESTURES AT THE **FLAMES** OVER WHICH THE CIMMERIAN LEAPS--

--SO THAT A SUDDEN FLASH OF **GREEN FLAME** BRIGHTENS THE HALL IN A SOUND-LESS PUFF OF EMERALD BRILLIANCE!

**CROM, MITRA, AND ISHTAR!**

THE UNCANNY RADIANCE SWIRLS ABOUT THOTH-AMON, EVEN AS CONAN HALTS TO SNATCH UP **LOUHI'S THRONE** AS A WEAPON...

BUT, EVEN THE BRONZED MONARCH'S **BLURRING SPEED** IS TOO SLOW!

**DAMN!**

NEXT INSTANT, THE MASTER SORCERER HAS **FADED** FROM SIGHT.

HIS MUSCLES TENSING, CONAN SUDDENLY RECALLS THAT HE HAD SEEN, OUT OF THE CORNER OF ONE EYE, THE WITCHWOMAN **LOUHI**-- HER ROBE YET AFIRE-- BEHIND HIM...

TURNING SWIFTLY, HE FINDS HER **STILL** BEHIND HIM...

...BUT NO LONGER A THREAT TO **ANYONE.**

IT IS YOUNG **CONN**, HOWEVER, FOR WHOM THE KING'S EYES DESPERATELY SEARCH:

RINGED ABOUT BY WITCHMEN, THE BOY HAS **INJURED** SEVERAL, HE SEES WITH FIERCE PRIDE.

THERE IS NO TIME TO **GO** TO HIM, HOWEVER -- AS A **SCORE** OF HYPERBOREANS EVEN NOW LEAP UP THE STEPS OF THE DAIS TOWARD **CONAN** HIMSELF!

THE **HEAT** REMAINING IN THE TOPPLED COPPER BOWL SEARS HIS FINGERS AS HE LIFTS IT OVER HIS HEAD WITH A MIGHTY EFFORT --

I FOUGHT YOU DOGS **FORTY YEARS AGO** AND SURVIVED --

-- AND, BY **CROM**, I'M A BETTER MAN **NOW** THAN I WAS **THEN!!**

ARRR

THEN, CONAN WHIRLS IN TIME TO SEE TOWERING NENAUNIR **FADE FROM VIEW** IN A SECOND FLARE OF SOUNDLESS GREEN FIRE!

THAT **MAGIC**, IT SEEMS, CAN BRIDGE THE VAST DISTANCES OF SPACE BETWEEN FRIGID HYPERBOREA AND FAR JUNGLED **ZEMBABWEI**.

**HUHN!!** THAT MUST BE HOW THOSE THREE DEVILS **GOT** HERE IN THE FIRST PLACE!

THEY'VE IM-**PROVED** ON THINGS, SINCE THE DAY WHEN THOTH-AMON HAD TO TRAVEL BY **BOAT** TO THE PICTISH WILDERNESS, BUT --

**CIMMERIAN!**

WHO THE **DEVIL** --?

**PRA-EUN!**

THE EASTERN MAGE IS A **SORRY** SIGHT, INDEED -- YET EVEN NOW, HIS **EYES** BLAZE WITH DEADLY POWER INTO **CONAN'S** --

-- AS HE EXTENDS A BURNED YET BEJEWELED **HAND!**

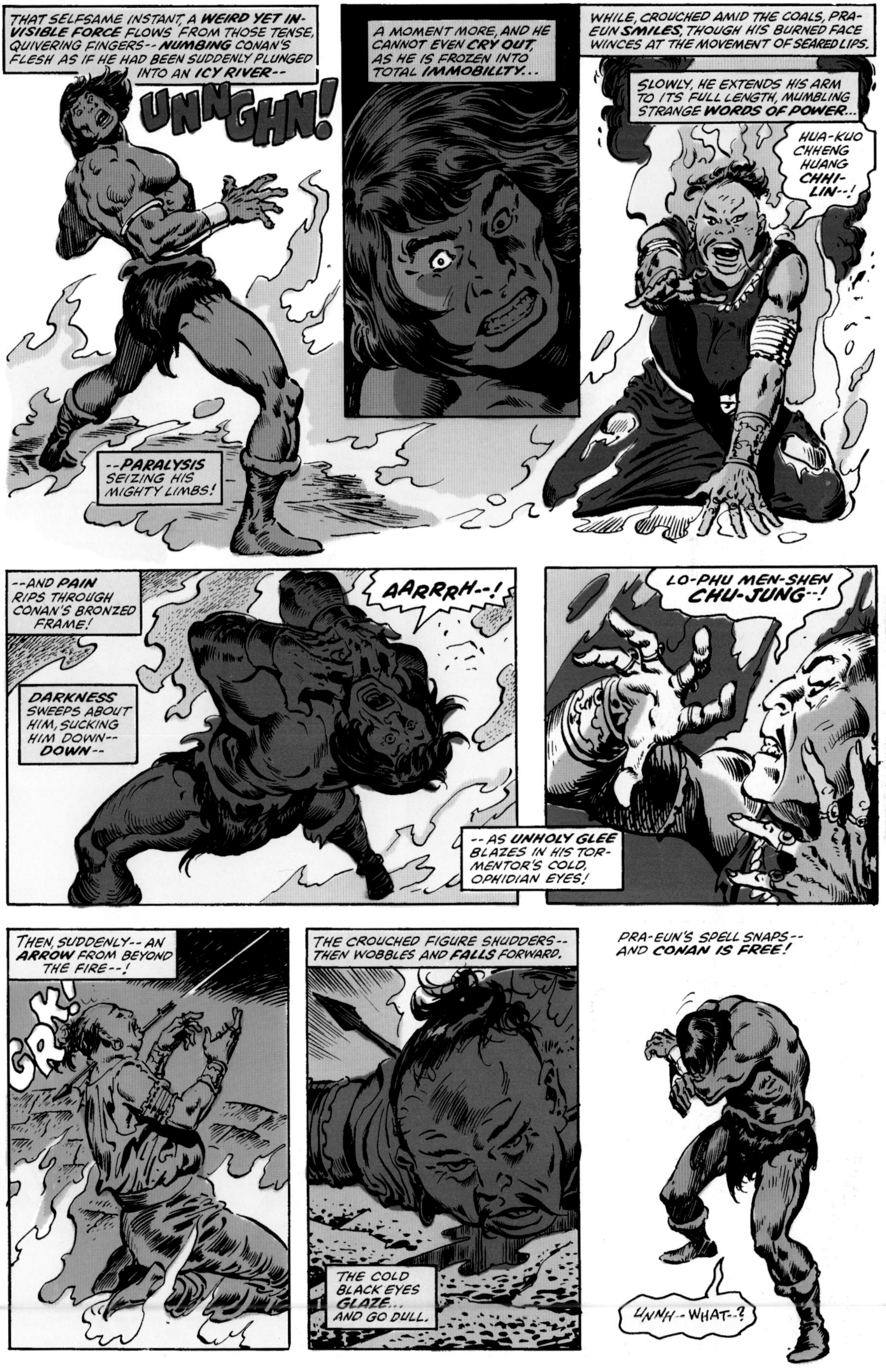
THAT SELFSAME INSTANT, A WEIRD YET INVISIBLE FORCE FLOWS FROM THOSE TENSE, QUIVERING FINGERS-- NUMBING CONAN'S FLESH AS IF HE HAD BEEN SUDDENLY PLUNGED INTO AN ICY RIVER--
UNNGHN!
--PARALYSIS SEIZING HIS MIGHTY LIMBS!
A MOMENT MORE, AND HE CANNOT EVEN CRY OUT, AS HE IS FROZEN INTO TOTAL IMMOBILLTY...
WHILE, CROUCHED AMID THE COALS, PRA-EUN SMILES, THOUGH HIS BURNED FACE WINCES AT THE MOVEMENT OF SEARED LIPS.
SLOWLY, HE EXTENDS HIS ARM TO ITS FULL LENGTH, MUMBLING STRANGE WORDS OF POWER...
HUA-KUO CHHENG HUANG CHHI-LIN--!
--AND PAIN RIPS THROUGH CONAN'S BRONZED FRAME!
AARRRH--!
DARKNESS SWEEPS ABOUT HIM, SUCKING HIM DOWN-- DOWN--
LO-PHU MEN-SHEN CHU-JUNG--!
--AS UNHOLY GLEE BLAZES IN HIS TORMENTOR'S COLD, OPHIDIAN EYES!
THEN, SUDDENLY-- AN ARROW FROM BEYOND THE FIRE--!
GRK!
THE CROUCHED FIGURE SHUDDERS-- THEN WOBBLES AND FALLS FORWARD.
THE COLD BLACK EYES GLAZE... AND GO DULL.
PRA-EUN'S SPELL SNAPS-- AND CONAN IS FREE!
UNNH-- WHAT--?

STILL REELING, THE WARRIOR-KING STANDS *GASPING*, AS STRENGTH AND VITALITY FLOOD BACK INTO HIS BENUMBED FLESH.

THEN, RAISING HIS EYES PAST PRA-EUN'S CORPSE, HE SEES--

EURIC!

*AYE* SIRE! IT WAS THE *RISKIEST* SHOT I EVER MADE, THE CROSS-BOW BEING AS IT IS...

BUT, *MITRA* WAS WITH ME!

AND BEHIND HIM COME A DOZEN MAIL-CLAD *KNIGHTS*-- AND A HUNDRED STOUT *GUARDSMEN*, WEARING THE LIVERY OF *TANASUL*.

*PROSPERO* HAS COME AT LAST!

AS DAWN ADDS ITS GLOW TO THE FLAMES, CONAN CARRIES AN EXHAUSTED HEIR-APPARENT FROM THE CASTLE...

WE CAME AS QUICKLY AS WE *COULD*, SIRE.

I KNOW, OLD FRIEND... AND MY *THANKS* FOR IT.

THANK THE GODS ALL THE WITCH-MEN WERE FIGHTING *YOU*, SO WE COULD *ENTER!*

FIGHTING ME-- AND MY *SON*, PROSPERO.

AND MY *SON!*

EVERY LAST MEMBER OF LOUHI'S FOLLOWING NOW AS DEAD AS SHE, THE GREAT KEEP COMES CRASHING DOWN IN *RUINS*...

*POHIOLA* IS NO MORE.

BUT ITS *EVIL* WILL LINGER IN MYTH AND FABLE AS LONG AS MEN DO LIVE!

SHALL WE GO *HOME* NOW, SIRE?

AYE... HOME TO *TARANTIA!*

I'VE HAD A *BELLYFUL* OF HUNTING-- AND OF *BEING* HUNTED.

*DEVIL* TAKE THESE HYPERBOREAN FOGS! I'VE THE *SOUR TASTE* OF THEM IN MY THROAT.

I WAS WONDERING, PROSPERO... HAVE YOU ANY MORE OF YOUR GOOD POITANIAN *WINE?*

AS I RECALL, AFTER THE HUNT, THERE WAS A *LITTLE* LEFT...!

NEXT MOMENT, CONAN BREAKS OFF, FLUSHING...

FOR, PROSPERO HAS BEGUN TO *LAUGH* UNTIL THE TEARS ARE POURING DOWN HIS CHEEKS... CUTTING RUNNELS THROUGH THE CAKED AND BLOODIED EARTH...!

HA HA HA!

NEXT ISSUE: **THE BLACK SPHINX OF NEBTHU!** ON SALE IN MARCH!

44

75¢ 2 JUNE 02480

**MIGHTIEST MONARCH OF A TIME-LOST LAND!**

# KING CONAN

DEATH BEYOND THE RIVER STYX!
**BLACK SPHINX OF NEBTHU!**

"Know, O prince, that the man called Conan was all things in his day: a thief, a reaver, a slayer... fierce sellsword and fiercer pirate... and finally, usurper king of proud, civilized Aquilonia, mightiest of Hyborian kingdoms... with his queen Zenobia at his side, and his son Prince Conn ripe to carry on the legend..."

—*The Nemedian Chronicles.*

# KING CONAN

Featuring The Epic Adventurer Created By **ROBERT E. HOWARD**

ROY THOMAS, SCRIPTER / EDITOR * JOHN BUSCEMA & ERNIE CHAN, ILLUSTRATORS * JOE ROSEN, LETTERER * G. ROUSSOS, COLORIST * JIM SHOOTER, CONSULTING EDITOR

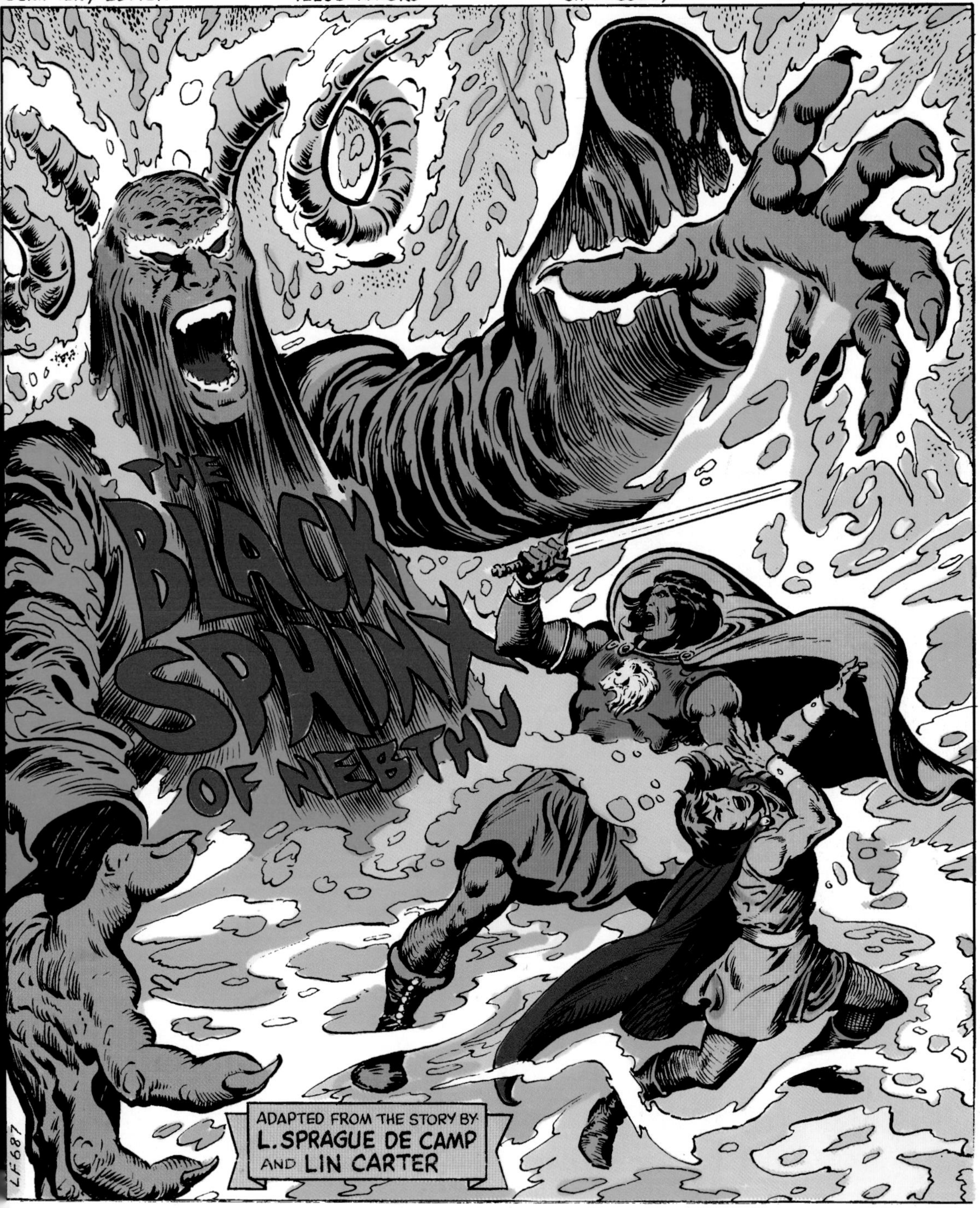
THE BLACK SPHINX OF NEBTHU
ADAPTED FROM THE STORY BY: L. SPRAGUE DE CAMP AND LIN CARTER
LF687

NIGHT LIES LIKE AN EBON PALL ON THE TRAMPLED, BLOOD-SOAKED EARTH OF ZINGARA.

THROUGH FLYING TATTERS OF MIST, AS THROUGH A RAGGED SHROUD, THE COLD WHITE SKULL OF THE MOON LEERS DOWN UPON A SCENE OF HORROR:

FOR, THE FOLLING, BARREN PLAIN THAT SLOPES DOWN TO THE SHALLOW ALIMANE RIVER IS ENCUMBERED THIS NIGHT WITH THE SPRAWLED CORPSES OF MEN AND THEIR MOUNTS.

IN SILENT HUNDREDS, DEAD KNIGHTS AND YBOMEN LIE, WITH DEAD EYES STARING UP INTO THE GRINNING JAWS OF THE MOCKING MOON...

...WHILE THE HIDEOUS MIRTH OF HYENAS RINGS WEIRDLY THROUGH THE STILL AIR.

NOT FOR NAUGHT IS THIS GRIM REGION CALLED... THE PLACE OF SKULLS.

HERE IT IS THAT THE BRIGHT IMPERIAL DREAMS OF PANTHO, DUKE OF GUARRALID, WERE DROWNED IN DARKNESS...

...HIS VAULTING AMBITION DRENCHED IN BLOOD.

THE THRONE OF ZINGARA LIES VACANT...AND FOR THAT PRIZE, PANTHO GAMBLED ALL:

FOR, AFTER EASILY CONQUERING THE WESTERN REACHES OF NEIGHBORING ARGOS--

--THE ZINGARAN NOBLEMAN SUDDENLY THRUST HIS ARMY DEEP INTO SUNNY POITAIN, SOUTHERNMOST PROVINCE OF AQUILONIA.

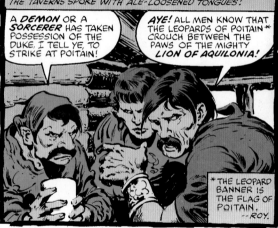

THE TAVERNS SPOKE WITH ALE-LOOSENED TONGUES:

A DEMON OR A SORCERER HAS TAKEN POSSESSION OF THE DUKE, I TELL YE, TO STRIKE AT POITAIN!

AYE! ALL MEN KNOW THAT THE LEOPARDS OF POITAIN * CROUCH BETWEEN THE PAWS OF THE MIGHTY LION OF AQUILONIA!

* THE LEOPARD BANNER IS THE FLAG OF POITAIN. --ROY.

NOR WAS **KING CONAN**, MONARCH OF THAT PROUDEST OF HYBORIAN NATIONS, SLOW TO TAKE UP THE HURLED GAUNTLET...

WHY DOES DUKE **PANTHO** STRIKE AT **POITAIN**-- WHEN HIS AMBITION MUST BE TO CONQUER **ZINGARA** ITSELF?

HE MUST MEAN TO SECURE HIS **REAR**, BEFORE STRIKING FOR **KORDAVA.** *

WELL, WHATEVER HIS MOTIVES, MY **IRON LEGIONS** WILL MAKE HIM KNOW HE'S **ERRED!**

* KORDAVA = CAPITAL OF ZINGARA. -- R.T.

AND WHEN THEY DID, CONAN HIMSELF RODE IN THE VANGUARD OF THE ATTACK.

ON THE GREEN PLAINS OF **POITAIN** DID THE ARMIES CLASH FIRST...

THE WILD ZINGARAN CHARGE **BROKE** LIKE THE SURF AGAINST THE STOLID PIKEMEN OF **GUNDERLAND**, AQUILONIA'S NORTHERN PROVINCE...

...WHILE THE SHAFTS OF CONAN'S **BOSSONIAN ARCHERS**, FROM HER WESTERN REACHES, MOWED DOWN THE INVADING KNIGHTS.

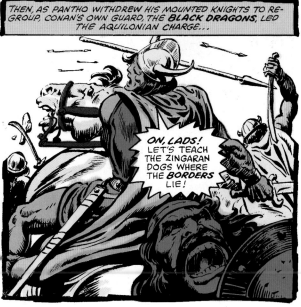

THEN, AS PANTHO WITHDREW HIS MOUNTED KNIGHTS TO REGROUP, CONAN'S OWN GUARD, THE **BLACK DRAGONS**, LED THE AQUILONIAN CHARGE...

ON, LADS! LET'S TEACH THE ZINGARAN DOGS WHERE THE **BORDERS** LIE!

FLEEING back across the Alimane to their homeland, the Zingarans were PURSUED by a vengeful CONAN...

...WHO CAUGHT UP WITH THE BATTERED, DEFEATED HOST AND CUT IT TO RIBBONS.

NOW, THE BANNER OF THE GOLDEN LION FLIES ABOVE A ROYAL TENT ON A KNOLL ABOVE THE DEATH-STREWN BATTLEFIELD...

MANY ZINGARANS DIED; SOME YIELDED; FEW ESCAPED...AND PANTHO'S DREAM DROWNED IN A CRIMSON SEA.

WHILE, INSIDE...

THIS WOUND NEEDS MUST BE SEWN, SIRE.

DO IT, THEN-- AND PAY NO HEED TO MY PLAINTS.

WITH THE DAWN, WE'LL DRIVE DEEPER INTO ZINGARA, TO SET A PUPPET ON THE THRONE TO END THIS DYNASTIC SQUABBLING--

--AND I INTEND TO LEAD THE ATTACK PERSONALLY.

GENERAL PALLANTIDES-- WHICH IS THE QUICKEST ROUTE FROM HERE TO STYGIA?

THAT ONE, SIRE.

AH, YES! I FOLLOWED IT HERE WHEN I FLED XALTOTUN'S WIZARDRY, SOME FIFTEEN YEARS AGO.*

*AS NARRATED IN OUR ADAPTATION OF THE NOVEL CONAN THE CONQUEROR. --ROY.

THERE'S SOMETHING ABOUT DUKE PANTHO'S INVASION THAT DOESN'T ADD UP, OLD FRIEND.

ONLY A FOOL OR A MADMAN WOULD HAVE HURLED AN ARMY AGAINST WAR-LIKE POITAIN, EVEN WITHOUT MY LEGIONS TO BACK IT UP,

I AGREE, SIRE, BUT WHAT--?

WE'LL NOT KNOW FROM THE DUKE, SINCE I SPLIT HIS SKULL TODAY--

-- BUT I KNEW HIM OF OLD, AND THINK HE WAS NEITHER MAD NOR FOOLISH.

I SUSPECT AN UNSEEN HAND BEHIND PANTHO'S MAD EXPEDITION-- A PLOT OF SOME KIND.

IN FACT, I SMELL... SORCERY.

LEAVE ME NOW. I WOULD THINK FURTHER ON THIS...!

IT IS THE KOTHIAN ADVENTURER **AMRIC THE BULL**, NOW OF THE BLACK DRAGONS, WHO GUARDS THE KING'S TENT THIS NIGHT...

THUS, HE IS THE **FIRST** TO SEE THE QUIET LITTLE MAN IN THE DIRTY ROBES WHICH ONCE WERE WHITE...

**FIRES OF MOLOCH!**

A **DRUID** OUT OF **PICTLAND**, OR I'M A EUNUCH!

HA HA HA! YOUR **SINS** HAVE FOUND YOU OUT, AMRIC OF KHORSHEMISH!

WHAT DO YOU **WISH** HERE, HOLY FATHER?

I WOULD FAIN SEE YOUR **KING** ERE I REST FROM MY LONG JOURNEY.

TELL HIM THAT **DIVIATIX**, CHIEF DRUID OF PICTLAND, AM COME WITH A **MESSAGE** FROM THE LORDS OF LIGHT...AND HOLD HIS DESTINY IN MY HAND.

A-AYE, HOLY FATHER...!

PROTECTING HIMSELF WITH THE SIGN OF MITRA, THE KOTHIAN MEEKLY TURNS TO OBEY THIS WITHERED-LOOKING OLD MAN.

AND, IMPROBABLY, THE WHITE DRUID SOON SITS BEFORE **KING CONAN** HIMSELF...

I HAVE **HEARD** OF YOU, DIVIATIX.

THEY SAY EVEN **DEKANAWATHA BLOOD-AX**, CHIEF OF THE PICTISH CONFEDERATION, GIVES WAY TO YOU.

AYE, THOUGH I AM **LIGUREAN**, NOT A TRUE PICT.

FROM THE GREAT GROVE AT **NUADWYDDON** HAVE I COME...

...OBEYING THE LORD OF THE GREAT ABYSS, **NUADENS ARGATLAM** OF THE SILVER HAND, TO **YOU**, THE GRIM GIANT THEY BROUGHT OUT OF WINTRY CIMMERIA LONG YEARS AGO, TO CRUSH **EVIL** IN THE WORLD'S WEST.

I CAME ON MY **OWN** POWER... BUT GO ON.

THE TOKEN THEY BADE ME BRING IS THIS SMALL **STONE TABLET**, OF WHICH I KNOW YOU HAVE HEARD... THOUGH NOT EVEN THE IRON-BOUND **BOOK OF SKELOS** DARED WHISPER OF IT...!

CROM! LET ME **SEE**...

FOR AN HOUR BY THE RINGED TIME CANDLE, CONAN LISTENS TO THE WHITE DRUID'S SLEEPY, WINE-BEFUDDLED DISCOURSE.

AT LENGTH, THE MOON SINKS...

AND, AS THE TRUMPETS SING AT DAWN...

*PRINCESS CHABELA!** I HEARD YOU AND YOUR CONSORT HAD ARRIVED LAST NIGHT.*

THEY ARE **WELL**, CO--MAJESTY. OLIVERO AND I HAVE COME TO EXPRESS OUR THANKS FOR YOUR PUNISHING OF THE AMBITIOUS **PANTHO**, AND--**OHHH!**

SAY NO MORE, DEAREST CHABELA.

IN FACT, I AM **GLAD** YOU'RE HERE... **BOTH** OF YOU...!

AND HOW FARE YOU AND OLIVERO'S **ELEVEN CHILDREN?**

*SEE **SAVAGE SWORD #40-43** FOR PRINCESS CHABELA, SOME TWENTY YEARS YOUNGER. --R.

WITHIN TEN MINUTES, CONAN HAS SETTLED THE LONG-VEXING PROBLEM OF THE ZINGARAN ROYAL SUCCESSION...

**RISE**, OLIVERO! YOU AND CHABELA ARE NOW **KING** AND **QUEEN** OF ZINGARA...

...UNDER THE OVER-LORDSHIP OF **AQUI-LONIA**, OF COURSE.

OF... COURSE.

THEN, DISPATCHING THE NEW TITULAR MONARCHS TO **KORDAVA** WITH A TROOP OF AQUILONIAN KNIGHTS TO SEE THE PAIR SAFELY INSTALLED...

...CONAN MOVES **SOUTHEAST** AT THE HEAD OF SIX THOU-SAND HORSES AND FOOT-SOLDIERS.

SOUTHEAST, ACROSS THE ARGOSSEAN BORDER... AND BEYOND THAT, TOWARD **STYGIA!**

AND WITH THEM COMES AN AGED, SHRIVELED **DRUID** IN A RATTLING MULE-CART.

ALONG THE WAY, HE MAKES PEACE IN THE NOW-FREED PROVINCES OF ARGOS WITH **ARISTO**, SECOND SON OF DEAD MILO... WHO QUICKLY PROCLAIMS HIMSELF **KING** OF THAT TROUBLED LAND.

HE SENDS OTHER HERALDS TO HIS VASSAL-KINGS OF **OPHIR** AND **KOTH**... AND ONE SECRETLY BACK TO HIS OWN CAPITAL OF **TARANTIA**.

THEN, HE DESCENDS LIKE A STEEL WHIRL-WIND UPON **SHEM**, WHOSE TERRIFIED CITY-STATES RAISE THEIR DRAW-BRIDGES IN **ALARM**.

TROCERO, COUNT OF POITAIN, IS DISPATCHED AHEAD TO PACIFY EACH AGITATED SHEMITISH KINGLET IN TURN...

...GENERALLY WITH GOOD AQUILONIAN SILVER.

LIKEWISE, THE FEW OF HIS SOLDIERS WHO MAKE FREE WITH EITHER SHEMITISH LIVESTOCK OR WENCHES...

...ARE HANGED IN FULL VIEW OF THEIR COMRADES.

AFTER ALL, THE LAST THING CONAN WANTS WHEN HE REACHES THE BORDERS OF STYGIA IS AN ANGRY, UNITED SHEM AT HIS BACK!

THEN, ONE NIGHT, AS THE ARMY CAMPS ON THE NORTHERN SHORES OF THE RIVER STYX, BOUNDARY OF SERPENT-RIDDLED STYGIA...

HO, THE CAMP!

IT IS YOUNG PRINCE CONN, AT THE HEAD OF A TROOP ON LATHERED HORSES.

AND HOW FARES YOUR MOTHER, THE QUEEN, BOY?

WELL, FATHER-- THOUGH SHE WAILED LIKE A WOUNDED BUFFALO WHEN SHE HEARD YOU WANTED ME HERE.

HOW LIKE A WOMAN! I REMEMBER MY OWN MOTHER, BACK IN CIMMERIA...

BUT, YOU SHOULDN'T COMPARE YOUR MOTHER TO A BUFFALO, BOY! THAT'S IMPERTINENT.

YES, SIRE.

BUT DO YOU REALLY WANT ME WITH YOU IN BATTLE?

CROM, BOY-- YOU'RE THIRTEEN ALREADY!

HOW CAN YOU HOPE TO HOLD THE THRONE WHEN YOU ASCEND TO IT, WITHOUT LEARNING THE ART OF WAR?

DID THE PRIESTS OF MITRA COME WITH YOU, AS I COMMANDED?

AYE, BEARING A LITTLE BOX COVERED WITH STRANGE WRITINGS... THOUGH THEY WOULDN'T TELL ME WHAT WAS IN IT.

DO YOU KNOW, FATHER?

THAT'S WHAT YOU MIGHT CALL OUR... SECRET WEAPON.

NOW, GET A GOOD REPAST AND A GOOD NIGHT'S SLEEP.

ERE DAWN, WE SHALL CROSS INTO STYGIA!

THE STYX: SOME CALL IT THE *RIVER OF DEATH,* AND TERM IT MORE THAN SIMPLY THE CLAMMY-VAPORED BORDER 'TWIXT STYGIA AND SHEM.

AND TRUE IT IS THAT THE RIVER'S WATERS ARE HOSTILE TO *HUMAN LIFE,* SO THAT HE WHO BATHES IN THEM IS SOON STRICKEN WITH A WASTING AND INCURABLE DISEASE...

...ASSUMING, OF COURSE, THAT THE HUGE *CROCODILES* DO NOT GET HIM FIRST.

NOW, IN THE HOURS BEFORE DAWN, KING CONAN LEADS THE WAY ACROSS THE *FORD OF BUBASTES* TO THE LOW, REEDY SHORE BEYOND...

*DISTURBANCES* IN STYGIA HAVE LED ITS RULERS TO DEPEND UPON *MOUNTED PATROLS* TO KEEP STRANGERS AT BAY...BUT IT SEEMS NONE OF THEM WILL CHALLENGE US.

WHEN YOU'VE CROSSED, EACH MAN WILL *DRY* HIMSELF AND HIS MOUNT... FOR SAFETY'S SAKE.

SIRE, I CAN HOLD MY SILENCE NO LONGER. *WHY* IN MITRA'S NAME ARE WE IN ACCURSED STYGIA?

BECAUSE THIS IS THE LAND OF OUR SECRET ENEMY...*THOTH-AMON!*

*THOTH-AMON!?* THAT STYGIAN WIZARD WE FOUGHT IN *HYPERBOREA* MONTHS AGO?*

*SEE ISSUE #1. --ROY.

*AYE,* TROCERO! THERE'S ONLY *ONE* THOTH-AMON, MY FATHER HAS EVER SAID.

WOULD TO CROM THERE WILL BE *NONE,* ONE DAY!

THE *WHITE DRUID* BORE ME WARNING OF HIS SCHEMES.

BUT WHAT HAS ALL THIS TO DO WITH DUKE PANTHO'S ATTACK ON *POITAIN?*

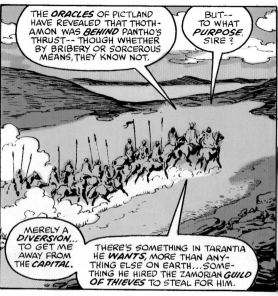

THE *ORACLES* OF PICTLAND HAVE REVEALED THAT THOTH-AMON WAS *BEHIND* PANTHO'S THRUST-- THOUGH WHETHER BY BRIBERY OR SORCEROUS MEANS, THEY KNOW NOT.

BUT-- TO WHAT *PURPOSE,* SIRE?

MERELY A *DIVERSION*... TO GET ME AWAY FROM THE *CAPITAL.*

THERE'S SOMETHING IN TARANTIA HE *WANTS,* MORE THAN ANYTHING ELSE ON EARTH...SOMETHING HE HIRED THE ZAMORIAN *GUILD OF THIEVES* TO STEAL FOR HIM.

54

BUT, THOTH-AMON *MISCALCULATED*-- NEVER DREAMING I WOULD SMASH PANTHO SO QUICKLY, NOR THAT THE ORACLE OF PICTLAND WOULD WARN ME OF THE PLOT.

HE STILL THINKS ME IN THE *NORTH,* CHASING THE ZINGARAN OVER HILL AND DALE.

DIVIATIX HAS KEPT OUR DESCENT INTO STYGIA *INVISIBLE* EVEN TO HIS MAGIC...OR SO HE *HOPES.*

SIRE-- WHAT *IS* THIS THING THE STYGIAN MAGE WANTS SO DESPERATELY?

*I* KNOW, COUNT! IT IS--

O KING! THE MEN ARE *READY* TO MARCH!

THEN GIVE THE *SIGNAL,* PALLANTIDES!

AS THE ARMY TURNS SOUTHWARD AND INLAND, A *CURSE* SEEMS TO OVERHANG THIS ANCIENT LAND... A SUBTLE THING, MOCKING WHISPERS IN AN EERIE WIND, THE HAUNTING SENSATION OF EYES AT THEIR BACKS.

CROSSING THE *BAKHR,* A SMALL TRIBUTARY OF THE STYX, THEY PASS A STYGIAN VILLAGE...

BUT ITS INHABITANTS ARE MORE INTERESTED IN *FLEEING* THAN IN WARNING THEIR DISTANT RULERS.

FATHER, I ALWAYS HEARD THAT THOTH-AMON DWELT AT AN OASIS CALLED *KHAJAR,* FAR WEST OF HERE.

NO MORE, LAD. NOW, HE MAKES HIS LAIR AT *NEBTHU.*

NEBTHU?

THE HEADQUARTERS OF THE *BLACK RING,* A WORLD-WIDE GUILD OF *EVIL MAGICIANS.*

I HEARD OF IT FIRST WHEN I SOUGHT THE MIGHTY TALISMAN CALLED THE *HEART OF AHRIMAN* IN THIS SINISTER LAND, YEARS AGO.*

IS THIS NEBTHU *WELL GUARDED,* SIRE?

*IN *CONAN THE CONQUEROR.* -- R.T.

MITRA KNOWS! IT LAY CRUMBLING INTO *RUINS,* THE LAST I HEARD, BUT I DON'T--

FATHER-- *LOOK!*

IS THAT-- *NEBTHU??*

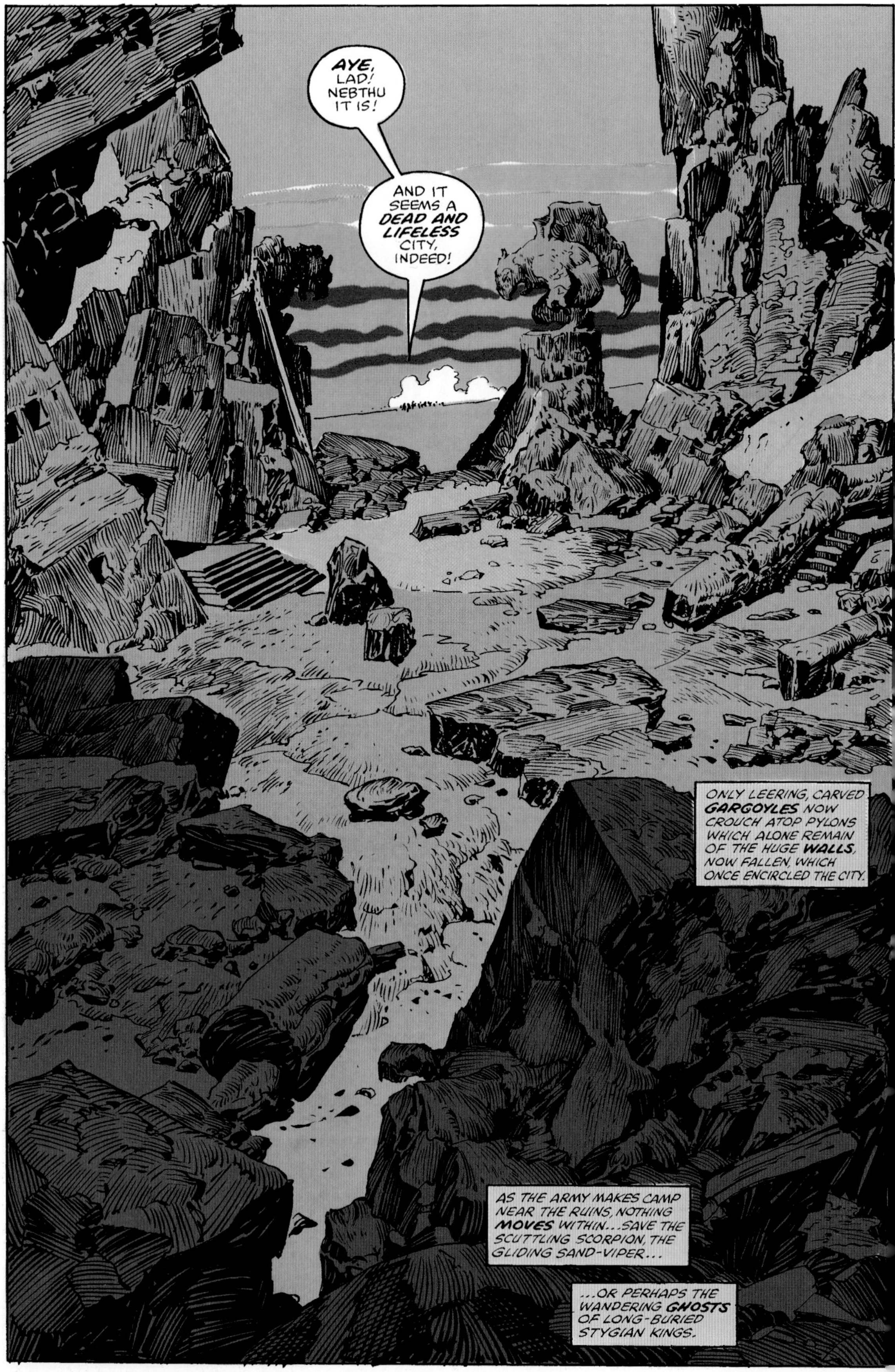
AYE, LAD! NEBTHU IT IS!
AND IT SEEMS A DEAD AND LIFELESS CITY, INDEED!
ONLY LEERING, CARVED GARGOYLES NOW CROUCH ATOP PYLONS WHICH ALONE REMAIN OF THE HUGE WALLS, NOW FALLEN, WHICH ONCE ENCIRCLED THE CITY.
AS THE ARMY MAKES CAMP NEAR THE RUINS, NOTHING MOVES WITHIN...SAVE THE SCUTTLING SCORPION, THE GLIDING SAND-VIPER...
...OR PERHAPS THE WANDERING GHOSTS OF LONG-BURIED STYGIAN KINGS.

LATER, WHEN SCOUTS HAVE REPORTED BACK THAT NO *AMBUSH* WAITS IN THE SAND-DRIFTED STREETS, CONAN LEAVES BEHIND THE COOKING-FIRES OF THE CAMP TO LEAD A TRIO OF STALWARTS INTO THE RUINED CITY...

*COME,* CONN... DIVIATIX... TROCERO!

I KNOW MY WARRIORS WON'T SLEEP EASILY IN SUCH A MAGIC-CURSED PLACE, SO I'LL LEAVE THEM *OUTSIDE* FOR THE TIME BEING.

FOR MYSELF, HOWEVER, I WOULD SEE THAT WHICH THE *SCOUTS* HAVE REPORTED.

JUST *TRY* LEAVING ME BEHIND, FATHER!

I DON'T FEAR ANY OLD *SUPERSTITIONS.*

YOUR SIRE KNOWS, LAD, THAT *SORCEROUS INFLUENCES* OFTEN LINGER ABOUT ANY ANCIENT RUIN...

...AND NOWHERE IS THAT TRUER THAN AGE-ACCURSED *STYGIA!*

ACCORDING TO THE SCOUTS, SIRE, THE GIGANTIC *IDOL,* OR *MONUMENT,* OR WHATEVER, SHOULD BE RIGHT PAST YONDER CRUMPLED PILLARS.

*THERE* IT IS, LORD OF AQUILONIA,

LET ME--!

STAY *BACK,* CONN, TILL I HAVE--

CROM, MITRA, AND VARUNA!

57

LIKE SOME **PRIMAL MONSTER** THE GREAT STONE STATUE CROUCHES AMID THE WASTE...

I-- I THOUGHT THE BLACK MAGICIANS OF THIS HELLISH LAND ALL WORSHIPPED **SET, THE OLD SERPENT.**

WHAT PIT-SPAWNED DEVIL-THING IS **THAT?**

I'D NOT THOUGHT EVER TO SEE ITS LIKENESS WROUGHT BY **HUMAN HANDS.**

BY THE HORNS OF CERNUNNOS-- 'TIS THE **GHOUL-HYENA OF CHAOS!**

LET US **BEGONE,** DIVIATIX...

...LEST THAT BLACK SPHINX HAUNT OUR **DREAMS** TONIGHT.

BUT ALREADY, CONAN KNOWS HE SPEAKS... TOO LATE.

SOON, AS THE COALS OF SUNSET SMOLDER OUT, **GLOOM** ENSHROUDS THE SANDS OF STYGIA BENEATH THE MOONLESS SKY...

...AS A CURIOUSLY SUBDUED HOST EATS ITS RATIONS AND SLUMBER...

...WHILE TWICE THE USUAL NUMBER OF **SENTRIES** ALERTLY PACE THE PERIMETER.

THE DESERT NIGHT IS EMPTY, DARK, AND SILENT... BUT **ALIVE.**

ALIVE... AND **WAITING.**

WEARY FROM MANY DAYS OF FORCED MARCHING, KING CONAN HIMSELF IS TOO *RESTLESS* TO SLEEP.

LONG AFTER MIDNIGHT, HE BROODS IN HIS TENT, SENSES TINGLING WITH ALERTNESS... AS IF HIS BARBARIAN INSTINCTS HAVE ROUSED HIM TO SOME *UNSEEN DANGER*

*DAMN* THIS LAND OF SNAKES AND SHADOWS!

RISING SUDDENLY, AS IF ON A SUDDEN *IMPULSE*, HE DONS MAIL-SHIRT, HELMET, AND SWORD...

THEN, UNLOCKING HIS STRONGBOX, HE TAKES OUT THE *SMALL BOX* WHICH THE MITRAIC PRIESTS BROUGHT HIM FROM TARANTIA.

SOON, *TROCERO* AND *PRINCE CONN* HAVE LIKEWISE BEEN SHAKEN FROM SLEEP, TO TRAIL IN HIS WAKE...

WHAT *IS* IT, FATHER? IS SOMETHING WRONG?

IN THIS THRICE-ACCURSED LAND, LAD, CAN YOU *ASK* THAT?

SILENTLY, THE TOWERING MONARCH STRIDES TOWARD THE TENT OF *DIVIATIX*.

BUT, ON ENTERING ALONE...

*ROUSE* YOURSELF, DRUID! I SENSE *DANGER*.

EYES...SHADOWS WITH EYES. THERE IS *EVIL* IN THE NIGHT...

*UP*, DIVIATIX! IS IT *DRUNK* THAT YOU ARE AGAIN?

I KNOW HOW YOU *PRIESTS OF PICTLAND*--

DRUNK? BY *MOTHER DANU*, KING, I HAVE SWILLED ENOUGH WINE TO SEND HALF THIS HOST STAGGERING...BUT I AM *COLD SOBER*.

CONAN SHIVERS AND WHIRLS, PEERING INTO THE DARKNESS.

BUT THERE IS NOTHING THERE...NOTHING BUT *SHADOWS*.

OUTSIDE IN THE DIM, STAR-FILLED NIGHT, *PALLANTIDES* HAS JOINED THE WAITING THREESOME...

WHAT IS IT, SIRE?

I KNOW NOT... BUT *SOMETHING.*

CROM CURSE IT, I CAN'T PUT A *NAME* TO IT, BUT SOMETHING'S *WRONG.*

SHALL WE ROUSE THE *HOST,* SIRE?

NOT YET. LET THE MEN GET WHAT SLEEP THEY *MAY,* EXCEPT...

PALLANTIDES, LEND ME TWO STOUT *MEN-AT-ARMS* WHO FEAR NEITHER GOD, MAN, NOR DEVIL!

WITHIN MINUTES, A PAIR OF YAWNING *GUNDERMEN* APPROACH WITH A CLINK OF MAIL...

YOU'LL DO. *COME!*

STRIDING DOWN THE SANDY LANE BETWEEN ROWS OF TENTS AND OUT TOWARD THE EDGE OF THE ENCAMPMENT, THE GROUP ENCOUNTER *AMRIC THE BULL*...

HO, MY BRAVE KOTHIAN! HAVE YOU SEEN ANYTHING AMISS?

NOTHING AT ALL, LORD KING, THOUGH WE'VE HEARD THE FAR-OFF YAPPING OF *JACKALS.*

ALSO, A FEW OF THE SENTRIES COMPLAIN OF... WELL, *SHADOWS!* SHADOWS THAT *WATCH* THEM.

SHADOWS WITH EYES! THEN MY VISION WAS *TRUE!*

SHADOWS, EH? THEY'LL BE STARTING AT *MICE* NEXT.

WELL, THESE LORDS AND I WILL SEE IF WE CAN *FIND* YOUR PROWLING SENTRIES, AMRIC.

YOU MAY GO.

AND NOT LONG AFTER...

FATHER-- *THERE!*

*FOOTPRINTS!* IT SEEMS WE HAVE A *SPY,* AFTER ALL!

FOR NEVER *YET* HAVE I HEARD TELL OF SHADOWS THAT LEAVE FOOTPRINTS IN SOFT SAND.

SIRE, SHALL I SOUND THE *HORN?*

FOR ONE SKULKING SPY? **NONSENSE,** MAN?

WE'LL TRACK THE ROGUE TO HIS LAIR **OURSELVES.**

ONE OF YOU GUNDERMEN-- GO TELL **PALLANTIDES** WHERE WE'VE GONE, AND BID HIM SEND SOME MEN ON OUR TRACK!

BUT TELL HIM THAT THEY SHALL **NOT** COME UP WITH US, UNLESS WE GET INTO TROUBLE.

I HOPE TO CATCH THE SLINKER **UN-AWARES**...AND THEIR CLATTER WOULD ALERT HIM A LEAGUE AWAY.

TIME ENOUGH TO SUMMON THE WATCH IF WE STUMBLE UPON A NEST OF THOTH-AMON'S **SNAKE-WORSHIPPERS!**

WITHOUT ANOTHER WORD, THE CIMMERIAN-BORN SOVEREIGN PLUNGES OFF IN THE DIRECTION WHERE THE FOOTPRINTS LEAD.

SOON, THE TRACK HAS LED THEM OVER THE DUNE AND **BEYOND SIGHT** OF THE CAMP.

COUNT TROCERO FEARS THE LONG MARCH WITHOUT OPPOSITION HAS MADE HIS MONARCH BOTH REST-.LESS AND **RECKLESS**...

BUT, WHO CAN ARGUE WITH **KING CONAN OF AQUILONIA?**

THEN--

SIRE-- **LOOK THERE!**

I **SEE** HIM, TROCERO.

OR DOES HE?

IS IT A BLUR OF STRAINED EYES-- A TRICK OF SHADOWS-- OR DOES HE GLIMPSE A **FORM,** HOODED AND CLOAKED ALL IN BLACK, FLITTING BEFORE THEM--

--MOVING OMINOUSLY TOWARD THE TOWERING *BLACK SPHINX OF NEBTHU?*

BETWEEN THE STONE MONSTER'S OUTSTRETCHED *PAWS* THE FIGURE RACES.

AND THEN, IT *MERGES* WITH THE BASALT, AND--

*FATHER!* IT VANISHED AGAINST THE *BREAST* OF THE IDOL!

YOU MUST *SHARPEN* YOUR EYE-SIGHT, LAD.

DON'T YOU SEE? THERE'S A *DOORWAY,* THREE MEN HIGH, IN THE MONSTER'S CHEST!

WHEN IT SHUTS, IT WILL *BLEND* WITH THE SOLID STONE-- AND WE'D BE HARD PUT TO *SEE* THE DOOR, LET ALONE OPEN IT.

BUT NOW, IT'S MERELY *CLOSING* SLOWLY, ON UNSEEN HINGES--

--NOR SHALL IT CLOSE *FURTHER!*

CONAN'S SWORD JAMMED INTO THE HAIRLINE CRACK, THE CLOSING *STOPS.*

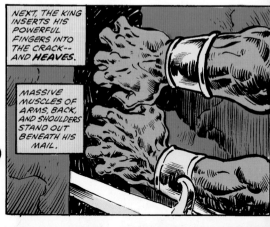

NEXT, THE KING INSERTS HIS POWERFUL FINGERS INTO THE CRACK-- AND *HEAVES.*

MASSIVE MUSCLES OF ARMS, BACK, AND SHOULDERS STAND OUT BENEATH HIS MAIL.

THEN-- THE PORTAL *OPENS* WITH A SQUEAL!

*UNNH!* THAT'S-- MORE *LIKE* IT!

NOW-- IF ONLY I CAN *HOLD* THE STONE DOOR--TILL EITHER ITS HINGES *GIVE*--

--OR ELSE-- IT *CRUSHES* ME-- TO A CRIMSON PULP--!

*SIRE!* THE PORTAL HAS *CEASED* ITS GRINDING!

BUT, HOW DID YOU *KNOW* IT OPERATED ON SOME SORT OF MECHANISM THAT WOULD *BREAK* WHEN STRONGLY ENOUGH RESISTED?

I DIDN'T.

NOW *COME*...

YOU, GUNDERMAN-- *THORUS,* ISN'T IT?-- PLANT YOUR *PIKE* TO HOLD THE DOOR OPEN, THEN RUN BACK TO CAMP!

TELL PALLANTIDES TO SEND A *WHOLE COMPANY* AFTER US!...

WE'LL *NEED* THEM!

YES, YOUR MAJESTY.

WITHIN THE SPHINX, THE FOUR STALWARTS FOLLOW A HIGH, WIDE CORRIDOR OF SOLID STONE... WARY EVERY PASSING INSTANT OF TRAPS AND PITFALLS.

DIVIATIX... YOU *HESITATED* BEFORE ENTERING THE SPHINX. WHY?

THE OLD SUPERSTITIONS DIE *HARD,* KING-- EVEN IN ONE WHO OFT HAS GLIMPSED THE NAKED SOURCE OF LEGENDS.

FOR UNTOLD AGES, IT HAS BEEN *FORBIDDEN* TO CARVE THE LIKE- NESS OF THE GHOUL-HYENA, YET THOTH-AMON AND HIS BLACK RING HAVE--

*HOLD,* DRUID! WATCH YOUR STEP, ALL!

FROM HERE, A BROAD STONE *STAIRWAY* DESCENDS.

LEADING-- *BENEATH* THE DESERT SANDS, FATHER?

AYE, LAD! THERE ARE SECTS WHICH SAY THAT HELL LIES IN SUCH A PLACE.

THEN WE'LL BE THE FIRST TO LEARN THE TRUTH.

DON'T LAG BEHIND, NOW; WE'VE BUT THE ONE TORCH.

BY MITRA, NO WONDER WE FOUND NO ONE IN THE CITY ABOVE.

THEY WERE ALL HIDING IN THIS MAZE.

AND A MAZE IT TRULY IS, SIRE-- LIKE THE ONE YOU TOLD ME OF IN BELVERUS, YEARS AGO.

WE'LL BE LUCKY TO FIND OUR WAY OUT AGAIN.

WE'LL NOT LEAVE SUCH A VITAL THING TO CHANCE, TROCERO.

THIS DAB OF PITCH FROM THE TORCH AT EVERY CHANGE OF DIRECTION WILL HELP US RETRACE OUR STEPS.

BUT, CROM TAKE ME-- EACH CHAMBER WE PASS THROUGH IS DESERTED-- BARE EVEN OF FURNISHINGS.

WHERE THE DEVIL ARE THE WIZARDS OF THE BLACK RING?

THE PROBABLE ANSWER COMES IN THE FORM OF... STILL ANOTHER STONE STAIRWAY.

BY THE GODS! ARE THERE LEVELS EVEN DEEPER THAN THIS?

IF THAT PHILOSOPHERS' NOTION BE TRUE, THAT THE WORLD IS ROUND, IT SEEMS WE'LL SOON COME OUT THE OTHER SIDE.

SIRE-- SHOULD WE NOT GO BACK FOR HELP?

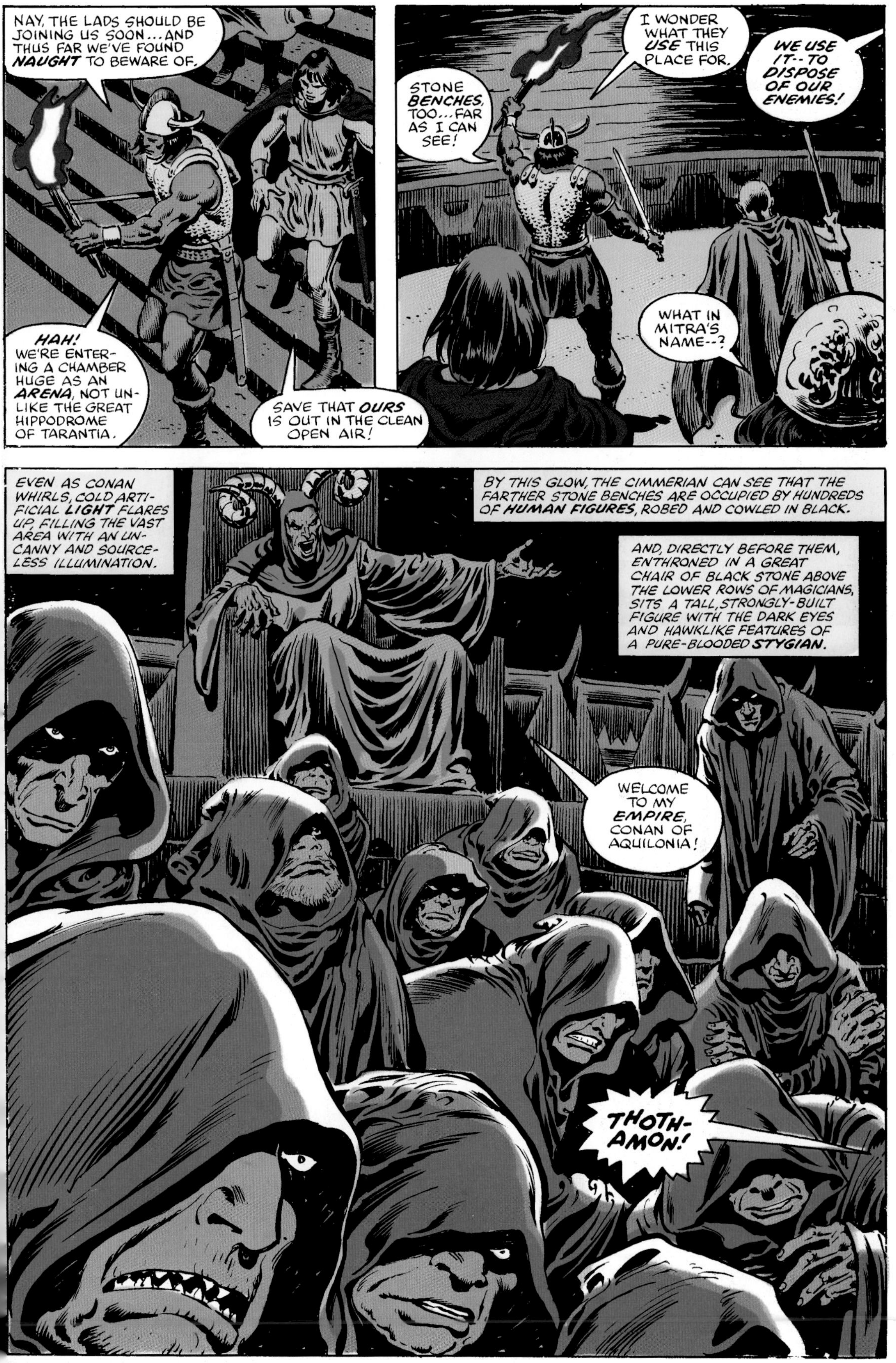
NAY, THE LADS SHOULD BE JOINING US SOON... AND THUS FAR WE'VE FOUND NAUGHT TO BEWARE OF.
HAH! WE'RE ENTERING A CHAMBER HUGE AS AN ARENA, NOT UNLIKE THE GREAT HIPPODROME OF TARANTIA.
SAVE THAT OURS IS OUT IN THE CLEAN OPEN AIR!
I WONDER WHAT THEY USE THIS PLACE FOR.
STONE BENCHES, TOO... FAR AS I CAN SEE!
WE USE IT-- TO DISPOSE OF OUR ENEMIES!
WHAT IN MITRA'S NAME--?
EVEN AS CONAN WHIRLS, COLD ARTIFICIAL LIGHT FLARES UP, FILLING THE VAST AREA WITH AN UNCANNY AND SOURCELESS ILLUMINATION.
BY THIS GLOW, THE CIMMERIAN CAN SEE THAT THE FARTHER STONE BENCHES ARE OCCUPIED BY HUNDREDS OF HUMAN FIGURES, ROBED AND COWLED IN BLACK.
AND, DIRECTLY BEFORE THEM, ENTHRONED IN A GREAT CHAIR OF BLACK STONE ABOVE THE LOWER ROWS OF MAGICIANS, SITS A TALL, STRONGLY-BUILT FIGURE WITH THE DARK EYES AND HAWKLIKE FEATURES OF A PURE-BLOODED STYGIAN.
WELCOME TO MY EMPIRE, CONAN OF AQUILONIA!
THOTH-AMON!

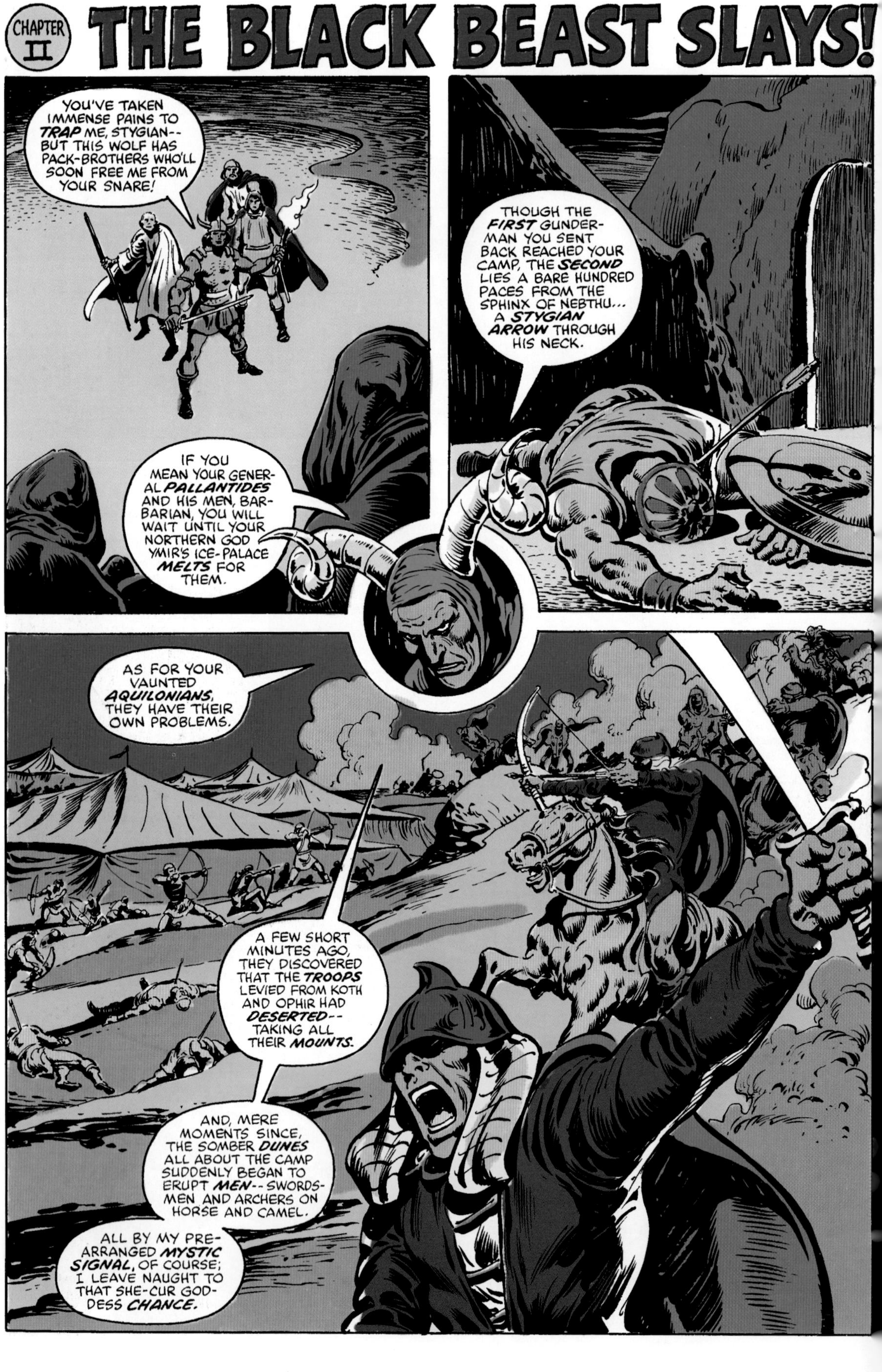
CHAPTER II THE BLACK BEAST SLAYS!
YOU'VE TAKEN IMMENSE PAINS TO TRAP ME, STYGIAN-- BUT THIS WOLF HAS PACK-BROTHERS WHO'LL SOON FREE ME FROM YOUR SNARE!
IF YOU MEAN YOUR GENERAL PALLANTIDES AND HIS MEN, BARBARIAN, YOU WILL WAIT UNTIL YOUR NORTHERN GOD YMIR'S ICE-PALACE MELTS FOR THEM.
THOUGH THE FIRST GUNDERMAN YOU SENT BACK REACHED YOUR CAMP, THE SECOND LIES A BARE HUNDRED PACES FROM THE SPHINX OF NEBTHU... A STYGIAN ARROW THROUGH HIS NECK.
AS FOR YOUR VAUNTED AQUILONIANS, THEY HAVE THEIR OWN PROBLEMS.
A FEW SHORT MINUTES AGO, THEY DISCOVERED THAT THE TROOPS LEVIED FROM KOTH AND OPHIR HAD DESERTED-- TAKING ALL THEIR MOUNTS.
AND, MERE MOMENTS SINCE, THE SOMBER DUNES ALL ABOUT THE CAMP SUDDENLY BEGAN TO ERUPT MEN-- SWORDSMEN AND ARCHERS ON HORSE AND CAMEL.
ALL BY MY PRE-ARRANGED MYSTIC SIGNAL, OF COURSE; I LEAVE NAUGHT TO THAT SHE-CUR GODDESS CHANCE.

THOTH-AMON CONTINUES: "ATOP THE HILLOCKS OF SAND, OTHER STYGIAN SOLDIERY APPEAR, SHOOTING *FIRE ARROWS* INTO THE CAMP.

"THE MISSILES TEAR COMETLIKE PATHS THROUGH THE DARK.

"FIRST ONE TENT, THEN ANOTHER *BLAZES UP.*

"YOUR GENERAL *PALLANTIDES,* NATURALLY, STRIVES TO RALLY YOUR STARTLED, CONFUSED FORCES...

STRIKE THE TENTS! *PUT OUT THE FIRES!*

*CENWULF!* WHERE IN HELL ARE YOU?

*HERE,* MY GENERAL! WHERE IS THE *KING?*

*MITRA* ONLY KNOWS! HE WENT OFF INTO THE DESERT, TRACKING A SPY.

SPREAD YOUR MEN AROUND THE PERIMETER AND *PICK OFF* SOME OF THOSE FLITTING BLACK-CLOAKS!

DETAIL A SQUAD TO BEAT DOWN THOSE DEVILS ON THE *DUNE,* WITH THE FIRE ARROWS!

*YES,* MY GENERAL.

*AMRIC!*

*HERE,* SIRE!

SPREAD THE MEN AROUND IN A *CIRCLE* OUTSIDE THE BOSSONIAN ARCHERS, KNEELING WITH PIKES READY TO STOP A *CHARGE!*

PILE *BAGGAGE* BEFORE THEM, AND HEAP SAND UPON IT FOR A *BREASTWORK..!*

"TAKEN ALL IN ALL, IT IS A *VALIANT* DEFENSE, I SUPPOSE... THOUGH WHO CAN TRULY SAY IF THE NAMES OF THOSE WHO SERVE AQUILONIA ARE ALREADY INSCRIBED IN THE *BOOK OF DEVILS?*

"*I* COULD, PERHAPS... BUT I SHALL NOT.

FOR *TOO LONG*, CIMMERIAN, HAVE YOU STOOD IN MY PATH!

I SAW YOU VENTURE INTO THE SOUTHERN LANDS FROM YOUR FROZEN NORTH, SOME *FORTY YEARS AGO*.

I SHOULD HAVE *CRUSHED* YOU THEN, WHEN YOU WERE YOUNG AND WEAK.

HAD I BUT KNOWN HOW YOUR POWER WOULD GROW, I WOULD HAVE STRUCK YOU DOWN WITH A BLAST OF MAGIC-- THAT *FIRST* TIME, WHEN YOU MEDDLED IN MY AFFAIRS IN THE *HOUSE OF KALLIAN* IN NEMEDIA...

...OR AGAIN, WHEN YOU SPOILED MY SCHEMES TO WREST THE *THRONE OF ZINGARA* FROM KING FERDRUGO'S FEEBLE GRASP.

GO ON, STYGIAN.

CROM KNOWS, YOU'VE *WAITED* LONG ENOUGH TO MAKE THIS SPEECH.

SO I HAVE, BARBARIAN... SO I *HAVE*.

THERE WERE *OTHER* OPPORTUNITIES, AS WELL.... FOR INSTANCE, WHEN I FIRST GLIMPSED YOU IN *COUNT VALENSO'S* STRONGHOLD ON THE WESTERN OCEAN...

...OR EVEN IN YOUR EARLIER YEARS OF *KINGING IT* IN AQUILONIA, WHEN I WAS ASCALANTE'S *SLAVE* IN TARANTIA.

THESE LAPSES, HOWEVER, SHALL NOW BE *CORRECTED*.

I FEAR YOUR SLINKING SERPENTS *LITTLE*, YOU STYGIAN SWINE!

WELL SAID, DOG OF A NORTHLANDER SAVAGE!

I ADMIRE YOUR *COOLNESS* AS MUCH AS MY FELLOW SORCERERS DEPLORE YOUR EFFRONTERY.

YOU WASTE *WORDS*, THOTH-AMON.

DESPITE YOUR SURPRISE ATTACK, I SUSPECT MY WARRIORS ABOVE ARE REAPING A *RED HARVEST*.

AH, BUT I DO NOT FIGHT WITH *SWORDS* ALONE, CONAN OF AQUILONIA...

...BUT WITH *SORCERY* AS WELL!

LANCING ACROSS THE ARENA, THE BOLT OF EMERALD STRIKES TROCERO'S *NAKED BLADE...*

MOTHER OF MITRA!

...SO THAT IT GLOWS *RED*, AND FALLS SMOKING FROM THE POITAINIAN'S HAND!

AND HE CAN BUT PUT HIS *BLISTERED FINGERS* IN HIS MOUTH, TO SOOTHE HIS PAIN.

AH YES-- *SORCERY!* I'VE ALWAYS LOATHED IT... STILL *DO.*

BUT SOME-TIMES, THE ONLY WAY TO *FIGHT* SORCERY...

...IS *WITH* SORCERY.

STEP FORWARD, HOLY FATHER...!

THE BLACK MAGICIANS ABOVE *RECOIL,* HISSING...

IT IS A *WHITE DRUID OF PICTLAND!*

IT IS INDEED.

UNLESS MY SENSES DECEIVE ME, IT IS NONE OTHER THAN *DIVIATIX.*

*"DIVIATIX!"* THE CRY ARISES FROM A HUNDRED THROATS; YET, AT A SIGNAL FROM THE PRINCE OF SORCERERS, THEY FALL SILENT.

THE PRESSURE OF SCORES OF *EYES* POUR DOWN UPON KING CONAN AND HIS TRIO OF COMPANIONS.

THE SILENT, CON-CENTRATED *POWER* OF THOSE BLACK, GLITTERING EYES IS *UNNERVING.*

SUDDENLY, A **COLDNESS** LIKE A SINISTER, BLEAK WIND FROM ONE OF HIS FROZEN NORTHERN HELLS BLOWS UPON THE MONARCH'S HEART-- HIS LIMBS GROW NUMB, HIS VISION BLURS--

MORE-- WIZARDRY--!

FATHER! CAN'T **BREATHE**-- I--

THEN, EVEN AS CONAN FEELS THE **IRON** DRAIN FROM HIS MUSCLES-- SENSES HIS KNEES NEAR TO **BUCKLING**--

COME, **NUADENS**-- COME **DANU**-- COME **EPONA**!

STAND **BESIDE** YOUR SERVANT, DIVIATIX!

THE GROUP- SPELL IS BROKEN.

NEXT MOMENT, THE MAGICIANS OF THE BLACK RING **SAG BACK,** THEIR CONCENTRATION SHATTERED...

...AND CONAN IS STUNNED TO SEE **FRESH YOUNG LEAVES** SPROUT ABRUPTLY FROM THE DEAD WOOD OF THE STAFF!

FOR HIS OWN PART, DIVIATIX **SWAYS,** CHUCKLING...AS IF ALL THE WINE HE HAD DRUNK THAT NIGHT HAS AT LAST CAUGHT UP WITH HIM.

HEH HEH HEH

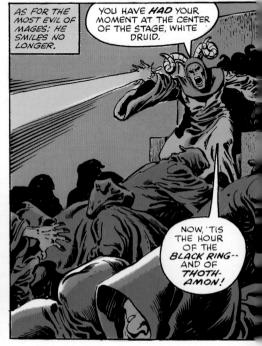

AS FOR THE MOST EVIL OF MAGES: HE SMILES NO LONGER.

YOU HAVE **HAD** YOUR MOMENT AT THE CENTER OF THE STAGE, WHITE DRUID.

NOW, 'TIS THE HOUR OF THE **BLACK RING**-- AND OF **THOTH- AMON**!

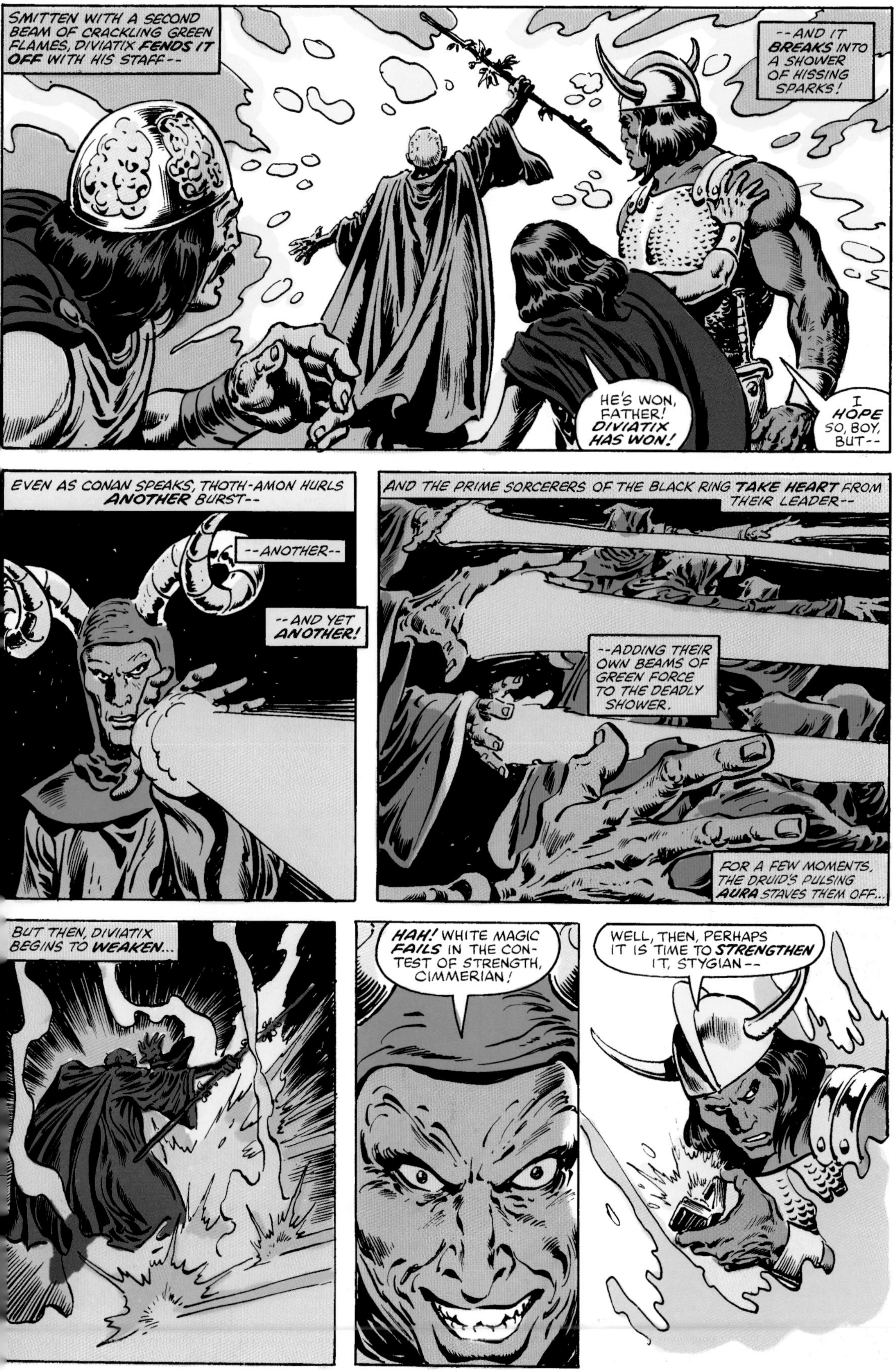
SMITTEN WITH A SECOND BEAM OF CRACKLING GREEN FLAMES, DIVIATIX FENDS IT OFF WITH HIS STAFF--
--AND IT BREAKS INTO A SHOWER OF HISSING SPARKS!
HE'S WON, FATHER! DIVIATIX HAS WON!
I HOPE SO, BOY, BUT--
EVEN AS CONAN SPEAKS, THOTH-AMON HURLS ANOTHER BURST--
--ANOTHER--
--AND YET ANOTHER!
AND THE PRIME SORCERERS OF THE BLACK RING TAKE HEART FROM THEIR LEADER--
--ADDING THEIR OWN BEAMS OF GREEN FORCE TO THE DEADLY SHOWER.
FOR A FEW MOMENTS, THE DRUID'S PULSING AURA STAVES THEM OFF...
BUT THEN, DIVIATIX BEGINS TO WEAKEN...
HAH! WHITE MAGIC FAILS IN THE CONTEST OF STRENGTH, CIMMERIAN!
WELL, THEN, PERHAPS IT IS TIME TO STRENGTHEN IT, STYGIAN--

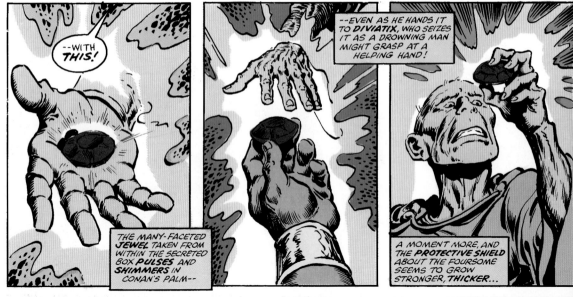

--WITH *THIS!*

THE MANY-FACETED *JEWEL* TAKEN FROM WITHIN THE SECRETED BOX *PULSES* AND *SHIMMERS* IN CONAN'S PALM--

--EVEN AS HE HANDS IT TO *DIVIATIX*, WHO SEIZES IT AS A DROWNING MAN MIGHT GRASP AT A HELPING HAND!

A MOMENT MORE, AND *THE PROTECTIVE SHIELD* ABOUT THE FOURSOME SEEMS TO GROW STRONGER, *THICKER...*

...AND A *GOLDEN FIRE* BLAZES UP TO SMITE THE DUSKY MAGICIANS!

AAIEEEE

HELP US, THOTH-AMON! *HELP US!*

SOME FALL BACK, SHRIEKING -- WHILE OTHERS SLUMP ALREADY IN UNCONSCIOUSNESS OR *DEATH.*

AND, AT LAST, THOTH-AMON *KNOWS:*

THE HEART!

*THE HEART OF AHRIMAN!*

AYE, STYGIAN DOG...

DID YOU REALLY THINK I'D VENTURE INTO YOUR DEN *WITHOUT* THE WORLD'S MIGHTIEST TALISMAN?

WHEN I LEARNED OF YOUR PLOT TO STEAL IT, I SENT *HERALDS* TO FETCH IT-- FROM THE VAULT WHERE IT HAS LAIN SINCE THE *DEATH OF XALTOTUN,* FIFTEEN YEARS AGO!*

AA AAAA

*SEE *SAVAGE SWORD* #10. --ROY.

*YOU* CANNOT USE THE GEM, BECAUSE IT CAN BE EMPLOYED ONLY FOR *GOOD*--

--SO YOU SOUGHT TO *STEAL* IT, SO IT COULD NOT BE USED *AGAINST* YOU!

BUT, YOU *FAILED,* THOTH-AMON! *YOU FAILED!*

AND NOW, *YOU ALONE* STILL LIVE, WITH FULL POSSESSION OF YOUR FACULTIES-- AND *SOON*, EVEN *YOU*--

YOU *FORCE* ME, SCUM OF A CIMMERIAN, TO PLAY MY *MASTERSTROKE!*

*FATHER SET!* SAVE THIS, THY SERVANT-- THAT HE MAY UNLEASH *BLACK DOOM* UPON THESE DEFILERS OF YOUR UNHOLY TEMPLE!

CONAN'S NAPE PRICKLES AS HE SEES A *SHADOW* GATHERING ABOUT THE STYGIAN-- LIKE THE COILS OF A GIGANTIC SERPENT--

AROUND AND ABOUT HIM THEY *DARKEN*, TILL HE STANDS CLOAKED IN UTTER GLOOM...THROUGH WHICH HIS *EYES* STILL BURN LIKE GLITTERING STARS OF OMINOUS FIRE...

IKHNA-APSU CHUNGAR SET!

BACK AND FORTH ACROSS THE SHADOWY IMMENSITY OF THE ARENA THE ALIEN WORDS ECHO...

NOW WHAT'S HE THINK *THAT* WILL--?

*THERE!* AT THE *FAR END* OF THE ARENA!

WE *SEE* IT, YOUNG PRINCE...

...AND WOULD TO ALL THE MANY-NAMED GODS THAT WE DID *NOT!*

AND THOTH-AMON... LAUGHS.

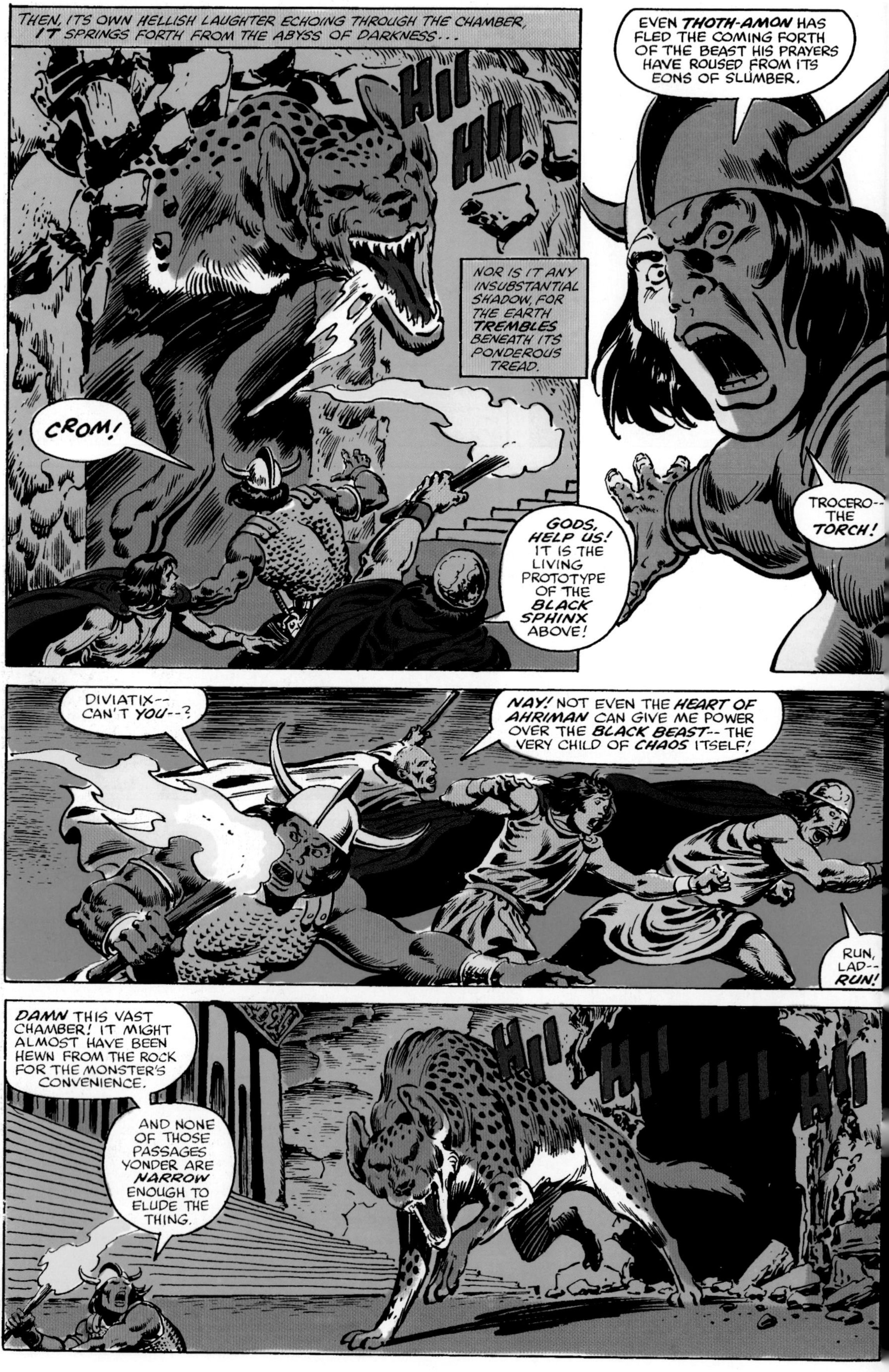
THEN, ITS OWN HELLISH LAUGHTER ECHOING THROUGH THE CHAMBER, IT SPRINGS FORTH FROM THE ABYSS OF DARKNESS...
HII HII.
NOR IS IT ANY INSUBSTANTIAL SHADOW, FOR THE EARTH TREMBLES BENEATH ITS PONDEROUS TREAD.
CROM!
GODS, HELP US! IT IS THE LIVING PROTOTYPE OF THE BLACK SPHINX ABOVE!
EVEN THOTH-AMON HAS FLED THE COMING FORTH OF THE BEAST HIS PRAYERS HAVE ROUSED FROM ITS EONS OF SLUMBER.
TROCERO-- THE TORCH!
DIVIATIX-- CAN'T YOU--?
NAY! NOT EVEN THE HEART OF AHRIMAN CAN GIVE ME POWER OVER THE BLACK BEAST-- THE VERY CHILD OF CHAOS ITSELF!
RUN, LAD-- RUN!
DAMN THIS VAST CHAMBER! IT MIGHT ALMOST HAVE BEEN HEWN FROM THE ROCK FOR THE MONSTER'S CONVENIENCE.
AND NONE OF THOSE PASSAGES YONDER ARE NARROW ENOUGH TO ELUDE THE THING.
HII HII HII HII

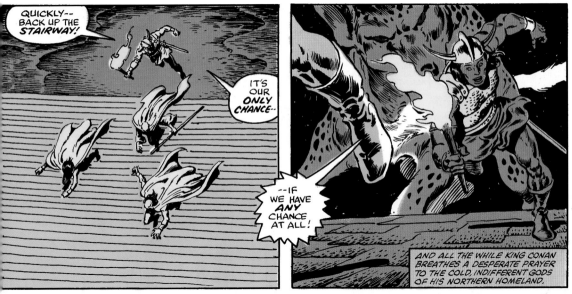

QUICKLY-- BACK UP THE **STAIRWAY!**

IT'S OUR **ONLY** CHANCE--

--IF WE HAVE **ANY** CHANCE AT ALL!

AND ALL THE WHILE KING CONAN BREATHES A DESPERATE PRAYER TO THE COLD, INDIFFERENT GODS OF HIS NORTHERN HOMELAND.

NOT THAT IT SEEMS TO BE DOING MUCH **GOOD.**

WHILE, **ABOVE:**

THE STYGIAN ARCHERS, MADE BRAVE BY THE SUCCESS OF THEIR SURPRISE ASSAULT, RIDE EVER **NEARER** THE DEFENDING HYBORIANS...

OCCASIONALLY, **TOO** NEAR...

...AND THE BOSSONIAN **LONGBOWS** TAKE THEIR TOLL ON THE MOUNTED STYGIANS, WITH THEIR SHORTER WEAPONS.

WHEN THE HEAVY AQUILONIAN SHAFTS STRIKE HOME, THEY PIERCE THROUGH MAIL AND CLOTH AND FLESH TO THE **VITALS.**

AT LENGTH, THE STYGIANS **RETREAT**, TO AWAIT THE ARRIVAL OF THEIR MIGHTIEST ALLY: THE **SUN**.

IN THE MORNING LIGHT, THE HORSE-LESS HYBORIANS WILL BE AT A GREATER DISADVANTAGE AGAINST THEIR MOUNTED **ATTACKERS**.

MEANWHILE:

STONE GRATES-- AND THE MASS-IVE PORTAL IN THE BREAST OF THE BLACK SPHINX SWINGS **OPEN**.

*UNNNHH--!*

FATHER-- I CAN STILL FEEL THE **GROUND** TREMBLE BENEATH US...!

**AYE**, CONN. THE BLACK BEAST IS STILL **AFTER** US.

AND-- LOOK **THERE**, ALL--!

THOTH-AMON MUST HAVE SUMMONED THE WHOLE ACCURSED **STYGIAN ARMY**!

THERE'S ONE OF ITS **GENERALS**, DOUBTLESS EXHORTING HIS FOLLOWERS TO DESTROY THE FILTHY FOREIGN WORSHIPPERS OF **UNCLEAN GODS**.

IF WE RUN FOR OUR CAMP, AND THEY SEE US, IT WILL BE THE **LAST**--

WE HAVE **NO CHOICE**, KING.

THE **VIBRATIONS** OF THE APPROACHING GHOUL-HYENA GROW STRONGER...

THEN, FOLLOW ME!

THERE'S A **GULLY** OVER THERE THAT--

JUST THEN, THE STYGIAN **REINFORCEMENTS** BEGIN TO MOVE OUT TOWARD THE AQUI-LONIAN CAMP.

AS THE FATES WOULD WEAVE IT, THEY'VE CHOSEN AN **ILL MOMENT** TO RIDE PAST THE **LEFT PAW** OF THE SPHINX...

FOR, AT THAT MOMENT, *UNSEEN* BY THE STYGIANS, ON THE *FAR* SIDE OF THAT STONE PAW--

*HURRY!* MAKE FOR THAT *GULLY!*

*ALL HELL'S* ABOUT TO BREAK LOOSE UP HERE!

AND, A FEW SECONDS LATER, AS THE *DUSKY* GENERAL PASSES THE *FRONT* OF THE IDOL--

--IT *DOES!*

O FATHER SET--

SSAAAAVE MEEEE!

77

FLINGING ASIDE THE CRUSHED AND CRIMSON BODY OF THE GENERAL, THE GREAT GHOUL-HYENA TURNS, TO *TOWER* FOR AN INSTANT OVER THE STYGIAN HOST-- LOOKING FOR ALL THE WORLD LIKE THE *LIVING CUB* OF THE STONE CREATURE IT RESEMBLES.

THEN, IT IS *AMONG* THEM--

HI!! HI!! HI!!

--AND THE AIR IS HIDEOUS WITH THE SHRIEKING OF MANGLED *HORSES*, THE AGONY AND TERROR OF BROKEN *MEN*.

THE STYGIANS, FOR THEIR PART, DO NOT LACK *COURAGE*...AND THEIR SECOND-IN-COMMAND ORDERS ONE DESPERATE *CHARGE*, HORRIFIED THOUGH HE BE.

BUT, THE BLACK BEAST SWEEPS HIS MEN TO EARTH WITH SLASHING *CLAWS* AND SNAPPING *JAWS* AS FAST AS THEY COME WITHIN REACH!

AT LAST THE SET-WORSHIPPERS GO MAD WITH *HORROR*, TRAMPLING ONE ANOTHER IN THEIR HASTE TO FLEE.

YET, AFTER THEM COMES THE *THING*.

EVER IT SLAYS... AND SLAYS... AND *SLAYS*.

AT LONG LAST, THE *SUN'S* GOLDEN DISC LIFTS ABOVE THE DESERT BEYOND THE BAKHR...

THE DARK MONSTER RAISES ITS **HEAD**, AT DAWN'S FULL LIGHT, FROM THE SLAUGHTER...

...**SHIVERING** STRANGELY AS THE SUN'S INIMICAL RAYS STRIKE IT...

...AND SQUEEZES ITS GREAT BULK BACK THROUGH THE HUGE **PORTAL** IN THE CARVEN SPHINX'S BREAST.

THEN IT IS **GONE**, AND THE VAST STONE DOOR BOOMS SHUT BEHIND IT.

WILL IT **RETURN**, DIVIATIX?

**NAY**, KING. NOT, AT LEAST, TILL **NIGHTFALL.**

WE'LL BE **READY** FOR IT THEN, EH, FATHER?

BITE YOUR TONGUE, LAD! WE'LL BE **FAR** FROM HERE, WON'T WE, SIRE-- IF WE CAN FIND SOME **HORSES**, THAT IS?

**AYE**, TROCERO. THE STYGIAN HOST MOSTLY FLED ON **FOOT**, THROWN BY THEIR MOUNTS AMID THE TERROR OF THE BLACK BEAST.

WE'LL GATHER UP SUCH OF THEIR HORSES AS **LIVE**.

BACK AT THE CAMP, BLOODIED BUT UNBEATEN, THE AQUILONIAN TROOPS CAN SCARCELY BELIEVE THEIR OWN **DELIVERANCE**...

...AND THEY HAIL CONAN AS THE **BRINGER** OF THE DARK MONSTER THAT SAVED THEM... WHICH, IN A SENSE, HE **WAS**.

ALL HAIL KING CONAN!

FIND **PALLANTIDES**, COUNT, AND ORGANIZE THE RECOVERY!

DIVIATIX AND I HAVE SOME **PLANNING** TO DO.

WE COME BY *CAMEL* AND ON THE BACKS OF STYGIAN *PONIES*-- BUT THOTH-AMON SHALL NOT ESCAPE US!

WELL, DIVIATIX... I SUPPOSE THIS IS WHERE WE LEAVE YOU TO YOUR *WINESKINS.*

AYE, KING! YOU KNOW ALL THAT *I* LEARNED LAST NIGHT, IN MY *VISION.*

THE HEART OF AHRIMAN SHOWED ME THAT THOTH-AMON HAS FLED *SOUTH-EAST,* NOW THAT THE BLACK RING IS DESTROYED --

--MAKING FOR THE MYSTERIOUS KINGDOM OF *ZEMBABWEI.*

THEN IT'S THERE, BY CROM, I'LL MAKE HIM EAT MY *SWORD.*

SPEAKING OF SWORDS-- PLEASE LEND ME *YOURS,* PRINCE CONN.

SURELY, BUT WHAT--?

WITH A NAKED FOREFINGER, THE DRUID SKETCHES A SERIES OF *RUNES* ON THE BARE BLADE.

THEY APPEAR AS IF BY--

*MAGIC,* OR I'M NOT KING CONAN'S SON!

BUT WHAT DO THEY *MEAN*?

SUFFICE IT TO SAY, LAD, THAT ONE OF THE *POWERS* IN LAST NIGHT'S VISION BADE ME WRITE THOSE WORDS.

IT WAS SAID THEY'D PROVE OF *USE* TO YOU, AND NOW, *FAREWELL.*

WE ARE READY TO *MARCH,* SIRE.

THEN GIVE THE *COMMAND,* PALLANTIDES.

WHITHER *AWAY,* O KING?

SOUTHEAST TO THE *JUNGLE LANDS*--

--AND TO THE *ENDS OF THE EARTH,* IF NEED BE!

AND THE TRUMPETS SING.

## RED MOON OF ZEMBABWEI!

75¢ 3 SEPT 02480

# KING CONAN

ALL NEW! A DOUBLE-LENGTH ACTION EPIC!

DRAGON-WINGS OVER ZEMBABWEI!

"Know, O prince, that the man called Conan was all things in his day: a thief, a reaver, a slayer... fierce sellsword and fiercer pirate... and finally, usurper king of proud, civilized Aquilonia, mightiest of Hyborian kingdoms... with his queen Zenobia at his side, and his son Prince Conn ripe to carry on the legend..."

—*The Nemedian Chronicles.*

# KING CONAN

Featuring The Epic Adventurer
Created By **ROBERT E. HOWARD**

# RED MOON OF ZEMBABWEI!

THE RAINY SEASON HAS COME TO UPPER ZEMBABWEI... BUT SO HAS CONAN OF AQUILONIA.

FOR MORE THAN A MONTH, THE CIMMERIAN-BORN MONARCH HAS DRIVEN HIS ADOPTED LAND'S HOST ON AND ON, FOLLOWING THE COURSE OF THE RIVER STYX SOUTH TOWARD ITS UNKNOWN SOURCE, TILL EVEN HIS OWN SON PRINCE CONN FEELS THE WEARINESS THAT COMES TO PURSUERS...

FATHER-- HOW MUCH LONGER BEFORE WE'RE OUT OF THIS VILE SWAMP?

MY TUTORS TAUGHT ME THAT ZEMBABWEI IS MARKED BY EVER-GLADE FLATLANDS IN THE NORTH-- NOT MARSHES.

THE BOUNDARIES OF KINGDOMS ARE SELDOM MARKED BY LINES, AS THEY ARE ON SCHOLARS' MAPS, CONN.

BUT, WE'LL REACH ZEMBABWEI'S BORDER SOON, AND HAVE DONE WITH THE SWAMPS OF SOUTHERN PUNT.

KEEP MOVING, ALL!

ROY THOMAS
WRITER / EDITOR

JOHN BUSCEMA
ARTIST

DANNY BULANADI
EMBELLISHER

JOE ROSEN
LETTERER

G. ROUSSOS
COLORIST

JIM SHOOTER
CONSULTING EDITOR

WHILE, JUST OUT OF EARSHOT...

LOOKS LIKE *RAIN*, EH, PALLANTIDES?

BY MITRA, TELL ME SOMETHING *NEW*, COUNT TROCERO!

IT'S RAINED EVERY DAY FOR THE PAST *TEN*, TILL I'VE GIVEN UP TRYING TO KEEP THE RUST OFF MY GEAR.

CURSE ME, BUT I WISH THAT OLD TOSSPOT OF A *DRUID* WERE STILL WITH US!

PERHAPS OLD *DIVIATIX* COULD HAVE *MAGICKED* US THROUGH THE AIR TO *OLD ZEMBABWEI*-- OR THE *FORBIDDEN CITY*, AS ITS VILE INHABITANTS DO CALL IT.

*ANYTHING* WOULD BE BETTER THAN SLOGGING THROUGH THIS INFERNAL *MIRE!*

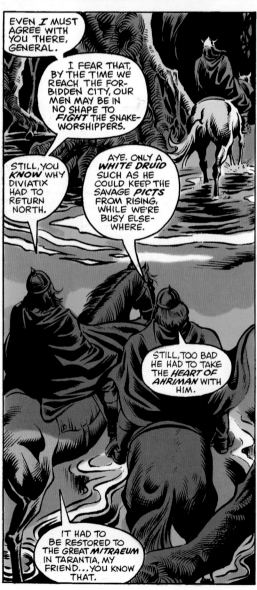

EVEN *I* MUST AGREE WITH YOU THERE, GENERAL.

I FEAR THAT, BY THE TIME WE REACH THE FORBIDDEN CITY, OUR MEN MAY BE IN NO SHAPE TO *FIGHT* THE SNAKE-WORSHIPPERS.

STILL, YOU *KNOW* WHY DIVIATIX HAD TO RETURN NORTH.

AYE. ONLY A *WHITE DRUID* SUCH AS HE COULD KEEP THE SAVAGE *PICTS* FROM RISING, WHILE WE'RE BUSY ELSEWHERE.

STILL, TOO BAD HE HAD TO TAKE THE *HEART OF AHRIMAN* WITH HIM.

IT HAD TO BE RESTORED TO THE GREAT *MITRAEUM* IN TARANTIA, MY FRIEND...YOU KNOW THAT.

BESIDES, THOUGH CONAN MAY BE THE MIGHTIEST *WARRIOR-KING* OF OUR AGE, HE IS STILL *NO WIZARD*...

...AND *ONLY* A MAGE, OR AT LEAST A DRUID, COULD HAVE USED THAT MAGICAL GEM EFFECTIVELY.

WELL, AT LEAST, BEFORE HE LEFT, DIVIATIX, USED HIS POWERS OF *DIVINATION* TO TELL US WHERE *THOTH-AMON* FLED TO.

NOT THAT THE STYGIAN HAD MUCH *CHOICE!*

THE LEADERS OF THE *WHITE HAND OF HYPERBOREA* AND OF THE EASTERN *SCARLET CIRCLE* WERE BOTH CRUSHED AT *POHIOLA*, MONTHS AGO.*

*ISSUE #*1.* --R.T.

86

THERE'S NO REFUGE *LEFT* FOR THOTH-AMON, SAVE ZEMBABWEI'S *FORBIDDEN CITY.*

AYE, FOR THERE HIS LAST ALLY--*NENAUNIR*, THE SUPREME WIZARD OF THE GOD *DAMBALLAH*, RULES COUNTLESS HORDES FROM HIS *SKULL THRONE*...OR SO IT'S SAID.

SMALL WONDER, AFTER HIS DEFEAT AT *NEBTHU,*\* THE MASTER OF THE BLACK RING FLED SOUTHWARD.

AND WHERE *THOTH-AMON* GOES, CAN *CONAN* BE FAR BEHIND?

\*LAST ISSUE. --ROY.

HALT, COMPANY!

*NIGHT* FALLS SWIFTLY-- AND WE CAN ADVANCE NO FURTHER!

"AT LAST WE'VE EMERGED FROM THAT TORTUROUS *SWAMP,*" BREATHES COUNT TROCERO.

SOON, UPON THE WATER-FREE *KNOLL* WHICH THE KING HAS CHOSEN, *COOKING FIRES* GLIMMER THROUGH THE GLOOM.

FATIGUED AQUILONIAN MEN-AT-ARMS FORGET THEIR GRUMBLING AND CURSING, EVEN THE BOTHERSOME INSECTS, AS THEY FILL THEIR GRUMBLING *BELLIES.*

MEANWHILE, AT THE FAR EDGES OF THE CAMP, *SENTRIES* PACE THE MARGIN OF THE SWAMP, EXCHANGING CURT PASSWORDS.

THERE ARE MORE VIPERS THAN ONLY *LEGLESS* ONES, IN THIS UNTAMED LAND SOUTH OF PUNT.

WHILE, WITHIN THE GREAT TENT AT THE CAMP'S CENTER...

I'M SORRY OUR SUPPLY OF BEER AND ALE HAS GIVEN OUT, YOUR MAJESTY, BUT I *BOILED* THE SWAMP WATER BEFORE I GAVE IT TO YOU OR THE ARMY...AS YOU *COMMANDED*.

DO THE MEN *GRUMBLE* ABOUT BEING FORCED TO DRINK BOILED WATER?

WELL...AS A MATTER OF FACT, MAJESTY...

*LET* THEM! THE PHILOSOPHER *ALCEMIDES* TOLD ME THAT WATER SO TREATED IS LESS LIKELY TO CAUSE *DISEASE*.

I'M NOT EDUCATED ENOUGH TO SEE THE CONNECTION, BUT ALCEMIDES IS A VERY *WISE* OLD MAN.

AH...*CONN!* HAVE YOU GROOMED THE MOUNTS ALREADY?

YES, FATHER. BUT YOURS TRIED TO *BITE* ME.

HORSES AREN'T VERY BRIGHT; YOU HAVE TO LEARN TO *HANDLE* THE BRUTES.

ANYWAY, HAVE SOME *FOOD*... SUCH AS IT IS.

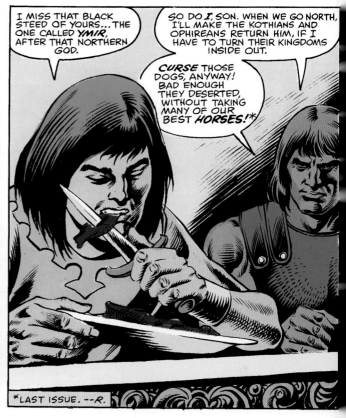

I MISS THAT BLACK STEED OF YOURS...THE ONE CALLED *YMIR*, AFTER THAT NORTHERN GOD.

SO DO *I*, SON. WHEN WE GO NORTH, I'LL MAKE THE KOTHIANS AND OPHIREANS RETURN HIM, IF I HAVE TO TURN THEIR KINGDOMS INSIDE OUT.

*CURSE* THOSE DOGS, ANYWAY! BAD ENOUGH THEY DESERTED, WITHOUT TAKING MANY OF OUR BEST *HORSES!**

*LAST ISSUE. --R.

88

MMMM... THAT BOILED STEAK ISN'T HALF BAD.

IS COUNT TROCERO STILL TRYING TO GET YOU TO SEND ME BACK TO *TARANTIA*, FATHER?

HE HAS AQUILONIA'S BEST INTERESTS AT HEART, AT LEAST AS HE SEES THEM.

*NONE* OF MY COUNCILORS LIKE THE IDEA OF BOTH MYSELF AND MY *HEIR* BEING HERE.

BUT, I THINK IT BETTER FOR THE NEXT KING OF AQUILONIA TO LEARN OF WAR-FARE IN THE *FIELD*, NOT FROM DUSTY BOOKS.

WELL, BEST *TOUR THE CAMP* BEFORE WE TURN IN; I'LL SLEEP BETTER IF I KNOW ALL IS SECURE.

BUT, IT SEEMS TO BE-- *EH*?

WHAT'S THAT SUDDEN *UPROAR*-- ARISING AT CAMP'S EDGE?

SOUND THE TRUMPETS, MAN! WE ARE ATTACKED!

BUT-- BY *WHOM*? I SEE NO ENEMY... NOR HEAR ANY HORSES' HOOVES.

CAN'T YOU *HEAR*? THAT *SOUND*-- COMING OUT OF THE VERY *SKY*!

WHAT BUT *SORCERY* COULD CAUSE SUCH A ROAR-- SO LOUD I CAN SCARCELY HEAR MYSELF *SHOUT*!

*STRANGE* SOUND! IT REMINDS ME, MORE THAN ANYTHING, OF THE *BOOM OF SAILS* AS THEY FILLED WITH A GUSTY WIND, BACK IN MY *PIRATE DAYS.*

BUT-- WHAT'S *THAT*, JUST ABOVE THE HORIZON-- HALF OBSCURED BY THE *MISTS*?

A'EEE! LOOK THERE-- AGAINST THE *CRESCENT MOON!*

WHAT IN *CROM'S* NAME--?

MEN-- RIDING FLAME-EYED **FLYING DEMONS** FROM HELL!

ARCHERS-- LOOSE YOUR ARROWS!

THAT'S A COMMAND YOU WON'T NEED TO GIVE **TWICE,** CAP'N!

THE BOSSONIAN ARCHERS, FROM THE WESTERN MARCHES 'TWIXT GREATER AQUILONIA AND PICTLAND, ARE THE BEST BOWMEN IN ALL THE WORLD --

--AS THE EERIE ATTACKERS SOON LEARN!

AAAIII! AAAIII!

MOTHER OF MITRA-- THE THINGS ARE **TAME!**

SHOOT THE **RIDERS** OFF THEIR BACKS, THEN -- AND WE'LL HAVE NO MORE TO **FEAR** FROM THEM!

EASIER SAID THAN *DONE*, MAJESTY!

IT'S HARD TO *SEE* A TARGET THAT SMALL WITH SO LITTLE MOONLIGHT-- LET ALONE *HIT* IT.

*UNNGN*

STILL, THE BELEAGUERED ARCHERS LOOSE VOLLEY AFTER VOLLEY INTO THE AIR--MANY OF WHICH MERELY REBOUND HARMLESSLY OFF THE LEATHERY *SCALES* OF THE WINGED MONSTERS--

--WHILE OTHER SWOOPING GARGOYLES GO FOR THE ARMY'S *HORSES*--

*WHNEEEE*

--AND STILL OTHERS SWOOP DOWN AMID THE *AQUILONIAN HOST ITSELF.*

FATHER-- WHAT--?

GET BACK OUT OF *HARM'S WAY*, BOY!

I'VE HEARD *LEGENDS* OF THESE REPTILES-- *WYVERNS,* THEY'RE CALLED--

AND, WHAT'S MORE TO THE *POINT*--

--IN MY DAY, I'VE FOUGHT DEVILS THAT WOULD MAKE THESE SEEM LIKE *TOADS* BY COMPARISON!

*CROM,* THOUGH-- I WISH, EVEN DYING, THEY MADE SOME *SOUND.*

MORTALLY WOUNDED NOW, THE FLYING CREATURE STAGGERS THROUGH THE AIR ACROSS THE CAMP, ITS DYING STRUGGLES KNOCKING OVER MEN LIKE TENPINS--

--ONLY TO CRASH INTO ONE OF THE CAMPFIRES, SCATTERING LIVE COALS IN A SHOWER OF SPARKS!

THE RIDER ON ITS BACK LEAPS OFF AT THE MOMENT OF IMPACT--

--BUT GOES DOWN, A MOMENT LATER, UNDER A SHOWER OF WEAPONS WIELDED BY VENGEFUL AQUILONIANS.

YYYIIIII

YOU SEE, MEN? THESE DEVIL-RIDERS ARE FIERCE-- BUT THEY CAN BE SLAIN!

BY CROM, WE'LL SEND THEM HOWLING BACK TO THOSE TOPLESS TOWERS THE LEGENDS TELL OF!

FOLLOW ME, LADS, AND WE'LL SOON--

AARRRAHH--!

TOO LATE HAVE THE BOOMING OF WINGS, THE RUSH OF DIS-PLACED AIR, WARNED HIM OF IMPENDING ATTACK...

AND NOW, THE EXTENDED CLAWS OF THE WYVERN CLOSE UPON THE CIMMERIAN'S BRONZE SHOULDER--

--TO BEAR HIM BODILY INTO THE NIGHT-SHROUDED SKY!

BELOW, HIS MEN CRY OUT IN ANGUISH AT THE SIGHT-- BUT THEY HAVE PROBLEMS OF THEIR OWN TO KEEP THEM BUSY.

THE **WIND**, TEARING PAST THE KING, HELPS HIM GATHER HIS SCATTERED WITS...

...AND HE REALIZES WITH A SILENT CURSE THAT THE **SWORD** HAS BEEN KNOCKED FROM HIS HAND.

HIS **DAGGER**, HE RECALLS, HE LEFT IN HIS TENT.

YET, AS HE GLANCES AT THE DARK **GROUND** SINKING AWAY BELOW HIM--

--HE SENSES THAT NEITHER SWORD NOR DAGGER WOULD DO HIM MUCH **GOOD** AT THIS MOMENT.

BEST **NOT** TO STRUGGLE OVERMUCH, LEST THE WYVERN **DROP** HIM TO HIS DEATH.

GOOD THING, AT LEAST, THAT HIS **MAILSHIRT** PROTECTS HIS HIDE FROM THE BEAST'S HUGE CLAWS.

THEN-- A SUDDEN **CRY** FROM BEHIND HIM--

**FATHER--!**

WHAT--?

**PRINCE CONN!**

NEITHER FATHER NOR SON CAN MAKE OUT ANY MORE WORDS, ABOVE THE BEATING OF GARGANTUAN WINGS...

...AS THE SECOND WYVERN DRAWS ABREAST OF THE FIRST.

THEN, **BOTH** SOAR AWAY, THEIR FELLOWS NOT FAR BEHIND.

BUT THEN, REASONS CONAN, WHY SLASH AT A LION'S **FEET**, WHEN YOU HAVE CUT OFF ITS **HEAD**... AND ITS **HEART**?

ON THEY FLY, INTO THE *NIGHT*... THOUGH THE WYVERN BEARING CONAN'S GREAT WEIGHT HAS DIFFICULTY MAINTAINING ITS ALTITUDE AND MUST OFTEN BE PRODDED.

WEARY WITH HIS EXERTIONS, AND FATALISTIC BY NATURE, CONAN EVEN *DOZES OFF* ONCE OR TWICE.

HOWEVER, AS THE TROPICAL *DAWN* SHINES ON HIS HEAVY EYELIDS --

CROM'S THUNDER!

--HE AWAKENS TO BEHOLD, HUNDREDS OF FEET BELOW, A *FANTASTIC CITY* LYING AMID CULTIVATED FIELDS, AND BORDERED BY A RIVER THAT SNAKES ITS WAY THROUGH DENSE JUNGLE,

ALL OF *STONE* IT IS... AND WITHIN ITS MEGALITHIC RAMPARTS RISE A SCORE OF STRANGE *TOWERS*, LIKE COLOSSAL CHIMNEYS.

CONAN NOTES AT ONCE THAT THEY HAVE NEITHER DOORS NOR WINDOWS...

...NOR EVEN *ROOFS*, FOR BLACK EMPTINESS YAWNS WHERE THEIR ROOFS WOULD HAVE BEEN.

HERE, IT'S SAID, MEN WORSHIP *SET*, THE OLD *SERPENT*, UNDER THE NAME OF *DAMBALLAH*, BEFORE AN ALTAR THAT OFT RUNS *CRIMSON*.

IT IS EVEN WHISPERED THAT, ON THE NIGHT OF HUMAN SACRIFICE, THE VERY *MOON* ITSELF BURNS RED WITH THE BLOOD OF THOSE WHOSE SOULS ARE OFFERED UP TO *DAMBALLAH*.

A GOOD PLACE, CONAN MUSES, FOR HIS *FINAL BATTLE* WITH THAT SNAKE-WORSHIPPING STYGIAN, *THOTH-AMON*.

RIGHT NOW, HOWEVER, IT IS A HOST OF ARMED, STALWART *ZEMBABWANS* WHO RING THE CITY'S CENTRAL PLAZA...

...INTO WHOSE *MIDST* HE AND YOUNG CONN ARE UNCEREMONIOUSLY *DROPPED*.

YOU *ALL RIGHT*, LAD?

YES, FATHER.

THIS DONE, THOSE TWO REPTILES RISE TO JOIN THE *OTHERS* OF THEIR KIND...

...AND CONAN REALIZES THAT THE FABLED "*TOP-LESS TOWERS*" ARE NAUGHT BUT *STABLES* FOR THE SCALY FLYING DEVILS.

SHALL WE TRY TO *ESCAPE*, SIRE?

YOU ARE BRAVE, BOY, BUT IT'S NOT LIKELY WE COULD--

THEY WOULDN'T BE *EXPECTING* US TO BE IN SHAPE FOR FIGHTING AFTER THAT LONG FLIGHT, AND WE MIGHT JUST--

WE MEET *AGAIN*, DOG OF CIMMERIA!

AYE-- FOR THE *LAST TIME*, JACKAL OF STYGIA!

AT CLOSE RANGE, CONAN SEES THAT *THOTH-AMON* IS STILL A POWERFUL, COMMANDING FIGURE... YET HIS KEEN EYES DETECT SIGNS OF ENCROACHING *AGE* IN THOSE HAWKLIKE FEATURES.

ARE THE STYGIAN'S POWERS AT LAST ON THE *WANE*, AFTER SO MANY LONG YEARS?

FOR THE LAST TIME, DID YOU SAY? *AYE, INDEED...*

...NOR SHALL WE FENCE WITH WORDS, BUT I WILL *SLAY* YOU NOW WHERE YOU STAND, AND YOUR *CUB* BESIDE YOU!

THE WEST SHALL YET FALL, AND *SET* SHALL AGAIN EXTEND HIS RULE OVER THE EARTH, WHEN I SIT AS *EMPEROR* IN TARANTIA, CAPITAL OF AQUILONIA!

THEY'D PUT A *REAL* SNAKE ON THE RUBY THRONE FIRST!

AS I SAID: I'VE NO TASTE FOR MINCING WORDS.

PREPARE FOR *DEATH!*

I'M AS READY AS I'LL *EVER* BE, SCUM OF THE SOUTH!

HALT!

BY THE SPAWN OF DAMBALLAH, STYGIAN-- DO YOU FORGET WHO *KINGS* IT HERE?

AND APPROACHING THE SKULL THRONE IS *NENAUNIR*, WIZARD-KING OF ZEMBABWEI... THE LAST OF THOTH-AMON'S SORCEROUS ALLIES.

I-- OF COURSE, BROTHER, *YOU* ARE SUPREME HERE; STILL, OUR MINDS HOLD THE SAME GREAT *SCHEME OF EMPIRE*, DO THEY NOT?

YOU SHALL RULE THE *SOUTH*... I, THE LANDS TO THE *NORTH*.

WE SHALL *DIVIDE THE WORLD*, WHICH SHALL HENCEFORTH GROVEL BEFORE *FATHER SET*...

BEFORE *LORD DAMBALLAH*, YOU MEAN-- WHOSE PROPHET AND VICAR ON THIS PLANE *I* AM!

WHAT? YOU *DARE*--?

YOUR DAY IS *DONE*, STYGIAN, AND I SEE NO REASON TO *SHARE* MY WORLD-EMPIRE WITH YOU WHEN IT'S WON.

MAYHAP I WILL APPOINT YOU *GOVERNOR* OF SOME MINOR PROVINCE... *IF* YOU BEHAVE YOURSELF.

AS FOR *YOU*, WHITE DOG, YOU HAVE INDEED *ERRED* BY DARING TO ENTER MY REALM.

I'LL *NOT* REPEAT THE MISTAKES MADE BY THE SORCERESS *LOUHI* IN HYPERBOREA, OR BY *THOTH-AMON* HIMSELF IN STYGIA.

I SHALL PRONOUNCE YOUR DOOM ON THE *NIGHT OF THE RED MOON*.

AT THAT TIME, YOUR BLOOD SHALL RUN SCARLET ON THE ALTARS OF THE SLITHERING GOD, WHILE YOUR SOUL GOES SHRIEKING FORTH TO FEED THE HUNGER OF *DAMBALLAH*.

AND JUST *WHEN* IS ALL THIS TO TAKE PLACE?

YOU ARE INSOLENT, AS ALWAYS.

*RIMUSH!* THE STARS ARE *YOUR* CONCERN. WHEN COMES THE NIGHT OF THE RED MOON?

IF SOME GOD INTER-FERES NOT, SIRE, IT WILL OCCUR SOME *TWELVE NIGHTS* FROM THE ONE JUST PAST.

SOME TIME LATER, A *SOUND* AROUSES THE HUGE CIMMERIAN FROM HIS EXHAUSTED SLUMBERS...

¿UNNNHHHNN--!

INSTANTLY, HE COMES TO FULL ALERTNESS, LIKE A JUNGLE BEAST.

WHO'S *GROANING*, THERE?

*SPEAK UP*, DAMN YOU, SO I CAN TELL WHERE YOU--

¿UHHHNN--¿ OVER-- *HERE*--

*FATHER-- WHO*--?

SOMEONE FROM A DARK *CELL* ACROSS THE CORRIDOR.

*NOW* I SEE HIM!

WHO ARE YOU? ARE YOU WELL ENOUGH TO *TALK*?

AYE...THOUGH EVERY BREATH... CAUSES ME *PAIN*...

YOUR *VOICE*-- IT'S LIKE--

AYE-- LIKE THAT OF *NENAUNIR*-- AND WELL SHOULD IT BE.

FOR, THIS DYING WRETCH...IS *MBEGA*... HIS *TWIN*...AND ONCE *KING* IN ZEMBABWEI...!

IF YOU SPEAK THE TRUTH, THEN THIS IS INDEED A *ROYAL* DUNGEON--

FOR, I AM *CONAN*, KING OF AQUILONIA, TO THE NORTH.

BUT, HOW DID YOU END UP IN *HERE*, IF YOU'RE--

FOR MANY YEARS... SINCE A PAIR OF *TWINS*...TAMED THE *FLYING ONES*, IN THE DIM PAST...

...IT HAS BEEN DECREED...THAT ZEMBABWEI MUST BE RULED...BY *PAIRS* OF TWINS.

WHEN ONE OF THE PAIR... WOULD DIE...THE OTHER WOULD *SLAY* HIMSELF... OR ELSE *BE* SLAIN.

AND THEN THE PRIESTS CHOSE *NEW* TWIN BOYS, I'LL WAGER.

YOU KNOW WELL... THE POWER OF PRIESTS, THEN.

AYE.....AND ALL WENT *WELL* WITH OUR YOUNG NATION... WHICH HAD SETTLED HERE...

"...UNTIL THE REIGN SHARED BY *NENAUNIR* AND *MBEGA*.

"MY BROTHER FELL IN... WITH A CULT OF *DEVIL-WORSHIPPERS*... WHOSE ANCIENT CULT DATES BACK TO *ACHERON*, KINGDOM OF SHADOWS.

"THE DEMON-GOD *DAMBALLAH*-- OR *SET*, AS THE STYGIANS CALL HIM-- PROMISED *GREATNESS* TO NENAUNIR IF HE AND HIS FOLLOWERS WOULD WORSHIP HIM.

"MY TWIN BROTHER'S CONVERSION... TORE THE PEOPLE INTO *FACTIONS*... AND, RATHER THAN SEE THE KINGDOM RENT ASUNDER AND DROWNED IN BLOOD...

"...I *SURRENDERED* MY SCEPTRE... TO NENAUNIR.

"BUT, THIS DID NOT SATISFY HIM... AND HE SET ABOUT TO *SLAY* ALL WHO WOULD NOT BOW TO DAMBALLAH.

"AND SO, WE OTHERS WERE FORCED AT LAST TO *REVOLT*... BUT BY THEN WE LACKED THE POWER TO OPPOSE HIM...

HE DARES NOT *SLAY* ME... SO HE IMPRISONED ME... FOR SUCH LITTLE LIFE AS I HAVE LEFT...!

YET, YOUR *FLOGGING*-- IT SEEMS *RECENT*.

WHEN LAST MY BROTHER PARADED ME BEFORE THE PEOPLE... I *SPAT* IN HIS FACE.

YOU STILL HAVE MANY *FOLLOWERS* IN THE CITY, THEN?

AYE... BUT THEY TOO WILL DIE... ERE LONG...!

Ten days later:

THE GODS PRESERVE US, PALLANTIDES-- HOW MUCH *FURTHER* TILL WE REACH THE FORBIDDEN CITY?

THE STENCH OF *ROTTING VEGETATION* WAS NEARLY--

I'D *LOWER* MY VOICE IF I WERE YOU, COUNT--

--UNLESS YOU WANT TO *WAKE UP* WHATEVER DEVILS DOUBTLESS SLUMBER BEYOND THOSE GREAT WALLS.

MITRA!

SENTRIES ON THE WALLS-- GUARDPOSTS ON THE TOWERS-- THIS WILL BE A *HARD* NUT TO CRACK.

AYE. IT WOULD TAKE *MONTHS OF SIEGE* TO FORCE AN ENTRY, AND BY THEN--

*DOWN*, TROCERO!--

THERE'S ONE OF THE BAT-WINGED HORRORS *NOW*-- BEARING ITS RIDER TOWARD THE CITY!

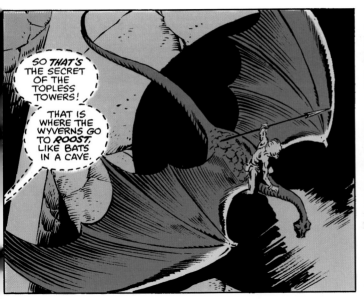

SO *THAT'S* THE SECRET OF THE *TOPLESS TOWERS!*

THAT IS WHERE THE *WYVERNS* GO TO *ROOST,* LIKE BATS IN A CAVE.

TO *MOLOCH'S FLAMES* WITH THE DEVILS!

WE HAVE A *KING* AND A *PRINCE* TO RESCUE!

I WONDER-- IF THEY'RE STILL *ALIVE!?*

*THAT* WE'LL FIND OUT ONCE WE'RE *WITHIN* THOSE WALLS.

YOU'VE HAD MORE EXPERIENCE WITH *SIEGES* THAN I, GENERAL-- BUT TO ME, THOSE WALLS LOOK *IMPREGNABLE.*

TO AN ARMY, YES-- BUT NOT TO A *LONE MAN.*

YOU HAVE A *PLAN,* THEN?

AYE, DO YOU RECALL THE ZINGARAN NOBLE, *MURZIO,* WHO RIDES WITH US?

THAT *SLY LITTLE TURNCOAT?* WHAT OF HIM?

A WEASEL, I AGREE-- AND I'VE LONG SUS-PECTED HE WAS ACTUALLY SPAWNED IN THE *GUTTERS* OF KORDAVA...

STILL, CONAN HAD HIS FRIEND *NINUS*...YOU KNOW, THAT THIEF-TURNED-PRIEST-OF-MITRA...* TEACH HIM MANY *TRICKS* OF HIS OLD TRADE.

AND MURZIO, IT'S SAID, PROVED AN APT *PUPIL.*

WHAT HAS THIS TO DO WITH GETTING INTO OLD *ZEMBABWEI?*

THERE'S ONE *UN-GUARDED* GATE TO EVERY GREAT CITY, COUNT--

*SAVAGE SWORD #40. --R.T.

--ITS *SEWERS!*

AND, IF THERE BE *ONE MAN* IN OUR ARMY WHO CAN WORM HIS WAY THROUGH YONDER GRILLE, IT'S *MURZIO OF ZINGARA...!*

GOOD! LET'S RETURN TO CAMP AND *INFORM* THE NOBLE MURZIO THAT--

OH NO-- *I* WILL BE THE ONE TO TELL HIM, MY FRIEND.

I NEVER *COULD* STAND ZINGARANS!

HOURS LATER, AS A PURPLE DARKNESS SPREADS ACROSS THE WALLS AND TOWERS OF THE FORBIDDEN CITY, A SLIM, GRACEFUL *FIGURE* SLIPS FROM THE EDGE OF THE JUNGLE...

...TO SWIM NOISELESSLY ACROSS THE RIVER, TOWARD THE REEKING RIVULET THAT FLOWS FROM THE GRILLE BENEATH THE FROWNING WALLS.

FOR A MOMENT THE FIGURE LINGERS, SEEKING AN ENTRANCE THAT WOULD NOT EXIST FOR A MAN LESS THIN.

THEN, IT SLIDES WITHIN... AND VANISHES FROM THE SIGHT OF ANY WHO MIGHT WATCH FROM THE SHADOWS.

MURZIO MAY OR MAY NOT POSSESS THE NOBLE BLOOD HE CLAIMS.

BUT, WHEN HE SWEARS FEALTY TO A KING, HE IS THAT KING'S MAN... TO THE *END*.

A few nights later...

NONE SLEEP IN THE CITY THIS EVENTIDE, FOR THIS IS THE NIGHT OF THE RED MOON.

WHEN THE OMINOUS CHANGE PASSES OVER THE HEAVENLY ORB, KING NENAUNIR WILL INVOKE HIS SINISTER SLITHERING GOD-- AND ALTAR AND MOON WILL REFLECT THE SAME SANGUINARY HUE.

TORCHLIT PROCESSIONS MOVE THROUGH THE NARROW, WINDING STREETS OF THE ANCIENT CITY...

...LIKE COUNTLESS FIREFLIES, DRAWN TOWARD A GREATER GLOW.

THE THUD OF DRUMS THROBS THROUGH THE HOT, BLACK AIR...

...AND WEIRD CHANTS ARISE, IN TONGUES NO WHITE OR YELLOW MAN KNOWS.

AND, THOUGH HE CANNOT SEE THE MOON FROM HIS WINDOWLESS CELL BENEATH THE STREETS OF OLD ZEMBABWEI!...

...CONAN KNOWS THAT IT IS FULL.

HE AND YOUNG CONN DO NOT SPEAK OF THE *DOOM* TO COME-- FOR THE CIMMERIAN HAS RAISED HIS SON NOT TO WASTE WORDS.

BETTER FAR, RATHER, TO TEST ONCE MORE ONE'S *STRENGTH* ON THE BARS OF THE PRIMEVAL CELL--

--TO *STRAIN*, ONCE MORE, WITH PALMS LONG SINCE *RUBBED RAW* WITH TRYING--

--WITH *SINEWS* THAT, IF THEY ARE NOT QUITE AS POWERFUL AS ONCE THEY *WERE,* ARE STILL THE *EQUAL* OF ANY *TWO* MEN HE IS EVER LIKE TO MEET.

OLD AND *CORRODED* THE BARS ARE--YET, THEIR VERY *THICK-NESS* HOLDS THEM IN THE PLACE THEY HAVE OCCUPIED FOR UN-TOLD EONS...

AND, THOUGH HIS *EARS* RING-- THOUGH HIS *FACE* BE CRIMSON WITH THE SUPERHUMAN EFFORT--

--AT LAST HE MUST *RELAX* HIS GRIP, PANTING FOR BREATH.

THE PREHUMAN BUILDERS OF THE CELL CALCULATED *WELL...*

--AND EVEN NOW, THEY ARE *BEYOND* THE *STRENGTH* OF ANY *MORTAL* MAN TO WRENCH ASKEW.

AT THAT INSTANT--WHEN DESPAIR STANDS POISED TO TRIUMPH OVER COURAGE--

EH? *WHO'S THERE?*

PERHAPS IN THE *LIGHT* YOU'LL KNOW ME, MY LIEGE.

*MURZIO!* IS IT YOU-- OR DO I *DREAM?*

HOW IN CROM'S NAME DID YOU GET IN *HERE*, REEKING LIKE A SEWER?

AND WHAT OF MY *HOST?* ARE THEY CAMPED NEARBY?

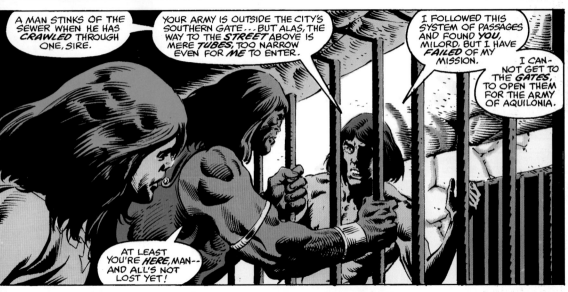

A MAN STINKS OF THE SEWER WHEN HE HAS *CRAWLED* THROUGH ONE, SIRE.

YOUR ARMY IS OUTSIDE THE CITY'S SOUTHERN GATE... BUT ALAS, THE WAY TO THE *STREET* ABOVE IS MERE *TUBES*, TOO NARROW EVEN FOR *ME* TO ENTER.

I FOLLOWED THIS SYSTEM OF PASSAGES AND FOUND *YOU*, MILORD, BUT I HAVE *FAILED* OF MY MISSION.

I CAN-NOT GET TO THE *GATES*, TO OPEN THEM FOR THE ARMY OF AQUILONIA.

AT LEAST YOU'RE *HERE*, MAN-- AND ALL'S NOT LOST YET!

HAVE YOU A *PICK-LOCK* SUCH AS NINUS TAUGHT YOU TO MAKE?

ONCE OUT OF THIS CAGE, WE WOULD AT LEAST HAVE A *FIGHTING CHANCE.*

A PICK-LOCK? AYE...

...BUT, CONFOUND IT, *FATHER NINUS* HIM-SELF COULD NOT SPRING THIS LOCK, SIRE.

I THINK IT *ACCURSED.*

THAT MAY WELL BE *TRUE*, MURZIO; I'D NOT PUT IT PAST THAT *STYGIAN JACKAL* TO HAVE ENCHANTED THE LOCK OF MY CELL!

BUT, THEN *WHAT* CAN--?

TRY THE LOCK ON THE CELL ACROSS THE WAY!

THE PRISONER THEREIN IS... A *FRIEND*, OF SORTS.

THE CHAINED MBEGA WATCHES IN IMPASSIVE SILENCE AS THE ZINGARAN SETS TO WORK ON THE LOCK OF HIS CELL...AND, ERE LONG...

IT'S *OPEN*, SIRE!

THANK *CROM!* NOW, *RELEASE* MBEGA-- HURRY, MAN!

UNNNHHNN--!

I'M-- SORRY FOR HOW MUCH THIS MUST *HURT* ONE WHO'S BEEN TORTURED AS YOU HAVE BEEN--

BUT, AT LEAST YOU'RE *FREE*, AND-- *MITRA*, BUT YOU'RE A BIG ONE!

I'LL BE ABLE-- TO STAND ON MY *OWN*-- IN A MOMENT.

NOT TO BE DISRESPECT- FUL-- BUT I'LL BE *GLAD* FOR THAT.

WELL DONE! YOU ZEMBABWANS BUILT A *STOUT* CELL DOOR-- BUT NO MATTER.

WHAT CAN- NOT BE CURED MUST BE ENDURED.

BUT... YOU FACE *DEATH*...

NOT FOR THE *FIRST* TIME, MY FRIEND.

WHAT MORE CAN I DO, MY LIEGE?

FIRST, SLIP ME YOUR *PONIARD*.

THE ZEMBABWANS HAVE STRIPPED ME NIGH NAKED...

...BUT AT LEAST THEY LEFT ME MY *BOOTS*.

CONAN... *I* KNOW THE WAY OUT OF THIS DUNGEON...

GOOD! HELP HIM, ZINGARAN.

MBEGA, THIS IS YOUR *LAST* CHANCE! IF YOUR FOLLOWERS CAN RISE BEFORE THE HOUR OF SACRIFICE AND OPEN THE *SOUTH GATE* TO MY ARMY, WE MAY *YET* OUTLIVE THE DAWN!

I SHALL DO... WHAT I *CAN*, MY NORTHERN FRIEND...!

AND NOW, AT LAST, FATHER SPEAKS TO SON...

BE OF *GOOD CHEER*, CONN.

ONE FRIEND *WITHIN* THE WALLS IS WORTH TEN THOUSAND LOCKED *OUTSIDE* THEM.

REMEMBER THAT *ALWAYS*.

I WILL, SIRE... ALWAYS.

SOON, THE TWO ROYAL CAPTIVES ARE ESCORTED BOUND FROM THE PITS BY A PARTY OF BLACK WARRIORS...AND OUT INTO THE GREAT *PLAZA* BETWEEN PALACE AND TEMPLE.

ALREADY THE *FULL MOON* RIDES HIGH IN THE SKY, ITS BRILLIANT LIGHT RENDERING THE STARS FEW AND WAN.

BUT NEITHER MOON NOR STARS NOR EVEN BLINDING SUN WILL EVER SHINE SO BRIGHTLY, IN CONAN'S STEEL-BLUE EYES, AS DOES HIS OWN *OFFSPRING* IN THIS TIME OF TRIAL.

WERE THE BOY NOT HIS OWN, NOR EVEN A PRINCE, THE CIMMERIAN CAN THINK OF *NONE* HE WOULD STAND BESIDE MORE *PROUDLY*.

NOW, KING AND HEIR STAND BEFORE THE GLYPH-CARVED *TEMPLE OF DAMBALLAH*...

...WHERE A STRANGE **ALTAR** OF BLACK MARBLE WAITS, BEFORE A SINISTER **SERPENT-IDOL** CARVED OF NIGHT-DARK BASALT, WITH GREAT RUBIES FOR EYES.

**SET**-- OR **DAMBALLAH**, AS THE **ZEMBABWANS** CALL THEIR SO-CALLED "SLITHERING GOD."

CROM...!

SWIFTLY, BOTH CAPTIVES ARE CHAINED AT THE BOTTOM OF THE BOWL-ALTAR...

...WHILE, ACROSS THE SQUARE, THE WASTED FIGURE OF **THOTH-AMON** STANDS BESIDE **KING NENAUNIR**.

THE SILENCE LENGTHENS, BROKEN ONLY BY THE MOAN OF THE NIGHT WIND OF THE NEARBY JUNGLE.

THEN, AS THOUSANDS OF HEADS TURN UPWARD, WITH DRAWN-OUT SIGHS --

-- A **RED SHADOW** WITH A CURVED EDGE BEGINS TO CREEP ACROSS THE FACE OF THE FULL MOON.

NOR COULD ANY MAN SAY **WHENCE** IT CAME.

FATHER--!

YES, LAD-- I KNOW! IT'S TIME TO **ACT**.

THESE **CHAINS**-- AND THE **WRIST-CUFFS**-- ARE MADE OF NEW BRONZE, THAT NO MAN'S SINEWS COULD BREAK --

BUT, THE *RING* SET IN THE MARBLE IS-- UNNNNH!-- WEAK FROM CENTURIES OF *RUST*--

--LIKE THE BARS-- OF OUR *CELL*--

--AND NOWHERE NEAR AS *THICK!*

*HAH!*

NOW-- GOT TO GET THE *OTHER* ARM FREE-- BEFORE THOSE DOGS LOOK DOWN-- AND SEE US!

≈UNNNFFH!≈

AT ANY SECOND, THE WARRIOR-KING HAS EXPECTED TO FEEL A *JAVELIN* STRIKE HIS BROAD BACK...

YET NOW, AS HE TURNS HIS EYES FOR AN INSTANT TOWARD THE ZEMBABWANS NEARBY...

...HE SEES THAT THEY ARE MERELY *WATCH-ING* HIM FREE HIMSELF, WITH STOLIDLY INDIFFERENT FACES.

AND EVEN AS HE LOOKS, THE *DRUM-MING* CHANGES ITS BEAT...

...AND A *BOOMING CHANT* ARISES FROM THE MASSED THOUSANDS.

DON'T WASTE TIME FREEING *ME*, FATHER! YOU MUST--

I MUST FREE MY *SON*-- OR I'M NO *MAN*, LIVE OR DIE!

SIRE--THAT *CHILL*--LIKE AN *ICY WIND* ON US! WHAT--?

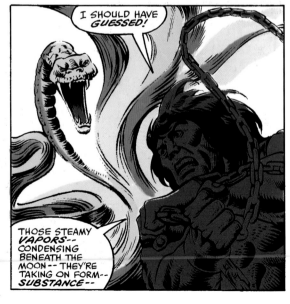

I SHOULD HAVE *GUESSED!*

THOSE STEAMY *VAPORS*-- CONDENSING BENEATH THE MOON-- THEY'RE TAKING ON FORM-- *SUBSTANCE*--

111

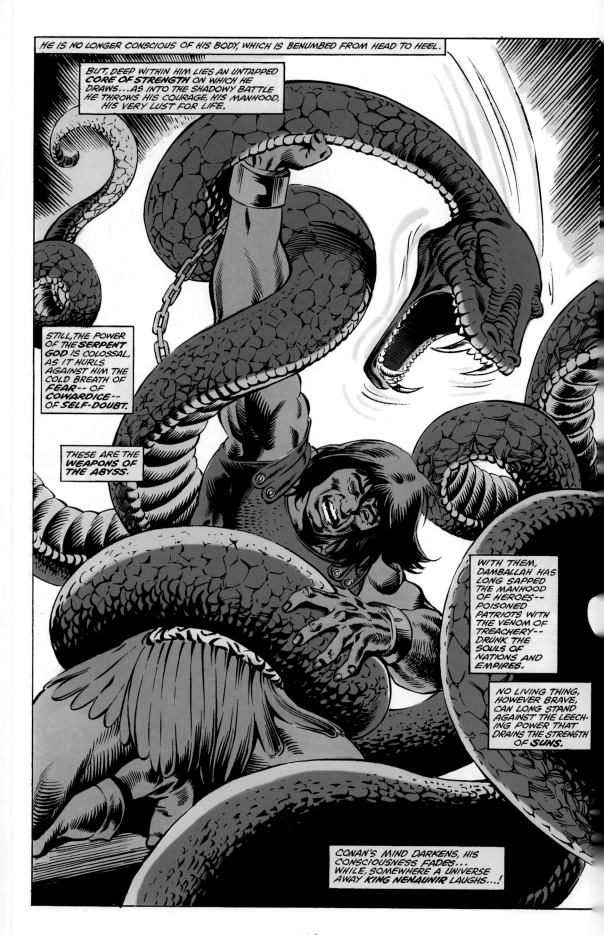

HE IS NO LONGER CONSCIOUS OF HIS BODY, WHICH IS BENUMBED FROM HEAD TO HEEL.

BUT, DEEP WITHIN HIM LIES AN UNTAPPED **CORE OF STRENGTH** ON WHICH HE DRAWS... AS INTO THE SHADOWY BATTLE HE THROWS HIS COURAGE, HIS MANHOOD, HIS VERY LUST FOR LIFE.

STILL, THE POWER OF THE **SERPENT GOD** IS COLOSSAL, AS IT HURLS AGAINST HIM THE COLD BREATH OF **FEAR** -- OF **COWARDICE** -- OF **SELF-DOUBT.**

THESE ARE THE **WEAPONS OF THE ABYSS.**

WITH THEM, DAMBALLAH HAS LONG SAPPED THE MANHOOD OF HEROES -- POISONED PATRIOTS WITH THE VENOM OF TREACHERY -- DRUNK THE SOULS OF NATIONS AND EMPIRES.

NO LIVING THING, HOWEVER BRAVE, CAN LONG STAND AGAINST THE LEECH-ING POWER THAT DRAINS THE STRENGTH OF **SUNS.**

CONAN'S MIND DARKENS, HIS CONSCIOUSNESS FADES... WHILE, SOMEWHERE A UNIVERSE AWAY **KING NENAUNIR** LAUGHS...!

AND THAT *GROSS*, IN-HUMAN LAUGHTER STIRS INTO ACTION ONE WHO HAS, TILL NOW, STOOD NUMB WITH SHOCK:

*PRINCE CONN,* WHO HAS NOT FLED AS ORDERED BY HIS FATHER--

--BUT WHO NOW RETRIEVES THE *DAGGER* FALLEN FROM HIS MIGHTY SIRE'S HAND--

--AND LOOKS ABOUT FOR A PLACE TO *SHEATHE* IT:

HIS QUICK MIND TELLS HIM THAT AGAINST THE COILS OF DAMBALLAH IT WILL BE TOO *LITTLE*... AND FAR TOO *LATE*.

BUT, THERE IS *ANOTHER* WHO CAN BE REACHED-- ONE WHO IS *MORTAL,* FOR ALL HIS SORCEROUS POWER:

*KING NENAUNIR!*

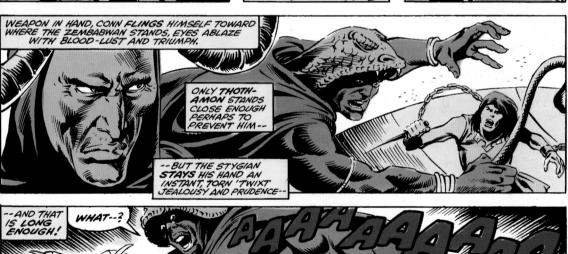

WEAPON IN HAND, CONN *FLINGS* HIMSELF TOWARD WHERE THE ZEMBABWAN STANDS, EYES ABLAZE WITH BLOOD-LUST AND TRIUMPH.

ONLY *THOTH-AMON* STANDS CLOSE ENOUGH PERHAPS TO PREVENT HIM--

--BUT THE STYGIAN *STAYS* HIS HAND AN INSTANT, TORN 'TWIXT JEALOUSY AND PRUDENCE--

--AND THAT IS *LONG ENOUGH!*

WHAT--?

AAAAAAAAAAAA

AS THE DAGGER PIERCES NENAUNIR'S HEART, THE *SPELL* THAT SUSTAINS DAMBALLAH ON THE EARTHLY PLANE IS *BROKEN*--

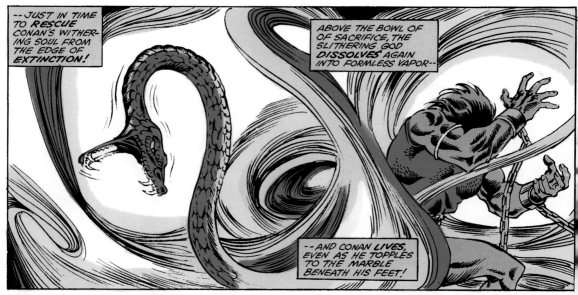

-- JUST IN TIME TO *RESCUE* CONAN'S WITHER-ING SOUL FROM THE EDGE OF *EXTINCTION!*

ABOVE THE BOWL OF OF SACRIFICE, THE *SLITHERING GOD* *DISSOLVES* AGAIN INTO FORMLESS VAPOR--

-- AND CONAN *LIVES,* EVEN AS HE TOPPLES TO THE MARBLE BENEATH HIS FEET!

*SLAY* THE MURDERING WHELP WHERE HE *STANDS!*

NO! SAVE HIM-- FOR THE *TORTURER!*

DO WHATEVER YOU *WANT!*

YOU WON'T BRING THAT *MAD DOG* BACK TO LIFE!

THEN, WHILE ZEMBABWAN SPEARS ARE *POISED*--

*HAIII--YAA!*

*AIIEEE!* IT IS THE *PARTISANS OF MBEGA!*

BUT-- HOW *DARE* THEY ATTACK US NOW?

THE QUESTION HANGS IN THE AIR, UNANSWERED-- AS THE CHARGING SPEARMEN STRIKE AT THE WORSHIPPERS OF DAMBALLAH FROM *ALL SIDES.*

THE DENSE, ORDERLY LINES OF NENAUNIR'S MEN SWIFTLY MELT INTO *CHAOS*--

--AS, LEADERLESS AND EASILY DISTINGUISHABLE BY THEIR PLUMED HEADDRESSES, THE FOLLOWERS OF NENAUNIR GO DOWN BY *SCORES!*

AS FOR KING CONAN:

ONE MOMENT, HE SEEMS TO SEE THE **RED MOON** LEERING DOWN-- AND HEAR **KING NENAUNIR'S** SATANIC LAUGH ECHOING THROUGH AN ABYSS OF NOTHINGNESS...

THE NEXT, THE DEATHLY **COLD** THAT NUMBS HIS BODY LESSENS...THE CRUSHING **PRESSURE** LIGHTENS...

...AND HE OPENS WEARY EYES...

...TO SEE THE **LAST REMNANTS** OF THE SLITHERING GOD **VANISHING** ABOVE HIS HEAD.

WHAT'S-- GOING ON--?

HE TURNS HIS HEAD AT THE SOUND OF A GREAT **UPROAR**--

--AND BEHOLDS WHAT MUST BE THE **FOLLOWERS OF MBEGA,** BATTLING WITH THE PARTISANS OF NENAUNIR.

**NENAUNIR!** EVEN AS HE STRUGGLES DIZZILY TO RISE, VENGEFUL EYES ALREADY SEEK OUT THAT VILE SERVANT OF DAMBALLAH.

THEN, ONLY A FEW PACES FROM THE EDGE OF THE MARBLE BOWL, HE BEHOLDS:

MANTLE OF MITRA!

THE CORPSE OF KING NENAUNIR-- STRUCK DOWN IN HIS HOUR OF TRIUMPH--

--MURZIO'S PONIARD GLEAMING IN HIS BREAST.

HIS FULL STRENGTH NOT YET RETURNED, HE IS FORCING HIMSELF ERECT, TO *JOIN THE BLOODY FRAY* --

-- WHEN HIS OWN *AQUILONIANS* ARRIVE, TO TIP THE TOPPLING SCALES OF BATTLE.

FOR KING CONAN -- AND YOUNG PRINCE CONN!

MOMENTS LATER, THE SQUARE RESOUNDS WITH THE CLATTER OF *DROPPED WEAPONS* ...

... AS THOSE WHO REMAIN ALIVE OF NENAUNIR'S MEN *SURRENDER*, SEEING FURTHER STRUGGLES USELESS.

THEN, AS CONAN STANDS ON HALF-NUMB LEGS ...

OH, FATHER -- *FATHER* -- I KILLED *NENAUNIR* --!

THE SNAKE-GOD WAS GOING TO *KILL* YOU -- I GRABBED THE KNIFE, AND --

EASY, LAD ...

IT'S ALL *OVER* NOW, AND YOU'LL ALWAYS REMEMBER THAT THE FIRST MAN EVER YOU SLEW ... WAS A *KING.*

BUT, IT APPEARS I WAS *WRONG* WHEN I SAID TO THOTH-AMON THAT OUR *FINAL BATTLE* WOULD BE FOUGHT AMONG THE TOP-LESS TOWERS ...

FOR, THERE HE GOES *NOW* -- NOR CAN ANY MAN STAY HIS *PATH!*

118

THE WYVERN IS BEARING HIM... SOUTH.

SOUTH: WHERE LIES NAUGHT BUT JUNGLE, AND THE EDGE OF THE KNOWN WORLD ITSELF.

THE STYGIAN MAGE IS *ALONE* NOW, HAVING LOST EVEN THE FAVOR OF HIS MERCILESS GOD.

WHERE ELSE CAN HE GO?

COME, BOY...LET'S FIND PALLANTIDES AND TROCERO...AYE, AND THAT SLY ROGUE *MURZIO*, WHOM I THINK I'LL MAKE A BARON!

BY DAWN, I'LL HAVE CROWNED *MBEGA* WITH MY OWN HANDS.

THEN, THE ARMY WILL REST HERE A WHILE, LICKING ITS WOUNDS.

AND *THEN*, SIRE?

HAH! YOU *KNOW* WHAT THEN MUST FOLLOW, CONN.

THEN IT'S *SOUTH*-- SOUTH TO THE *WORLD'S EDGE*, WHERE ON A NAMELESS BEACH THAT FRONTS AN UNKNOWN SEA, I'LL CLOSE WITH THOTH-AMON FOR THE *ULTIMATE BATTLE*!

CROM, BUT IT FEELS GOOD TO BE *ALIVE*!!

NEXT: SHADOWS IN THE SKULL! CIMMERIAN VS. STYGIAN-- TO THE DEATH!

75¢
CC
4
DEC
02480

TM

# MIGHTIEST MONARCH OF A TIME-LOST LAND!

# KING CONAN

THE SWORD-AND-
SORCERY SAGA THAT
HAD TO BE TOLD!
## CONAN vs.
## THOTH-AMON
--TO THE
## DEATH!

"Know, O prince, that the man called Conan was all things in his day: a thief, a reaver, a slayer... fierce sellsword and fiercer pirate... and finally, usurper king of proud, civilized Aquilonia, mightiest of Hyborian kingdoms... with his queen Zenobia at his side, and his son Prince Conn ripe to carry on the legend..."

—The Nemedian Chronicles.

# KING CONAN

Featuring The Epic Adventurer Created By **ROBERT E. HOWARD**

# SHADOWS IN THE SKULL!

ADAPTED FROM THE STORY BY
**L. SPRAGUE DE CAMP & LIN CARTER**

FEATURING THE HERO CREATED BY
**ROBERT E. HOWARD**

IN THE HEART OF *ZEMBABWEI*, CONAN OF AQUILONIA AND THE NEWLY-CROWNED *KING MBEGA* BASK ANXIOUSLY IN THE CRIMSON GLOW OF SMOLDERING COALS AS *RIMUSH*, ROYAL SOOTHSAYER OF THIS BLACK KINGDOM, COMPLETES HIS MYSTIC LIBATIONS...

BY THROBBING HEART OF *IBIS*... BY THE *ADDER'S* FORKED TONGUE... BY THE BLOOD OF THE *BULL-APE*...

...SHOW US, O GODS OF ZEMBABWEI, WHITHER HAS FLED THE STYGIAN WIZARD *THOTH-AMON*, MOST EVIL MAGE OF ALL...!

ROY THOMAS
WRITER/ EDITOR

JOHN BUSCEMA
ARTIST/ ILLUSTRATOR

DANNY BULANADI
INKER/ EMBELLISHER

JOE ROSEN
LETTERER

G. ROUSSOS
COLORIST

JIM SHOOTER
EDITOR-IN-CHIEF

AT LAST, KING CONAN STIRS RESTLESSLY...

*ENOUGH* OF THIS *MUMMERY!* YOUR GODS HEAR YOU NO MORE THAN *CROM* WOULD LISTEN TO ME.

MBEGA, GIVE ME A LEGION OF YOUR *WARRIORS*, AND I'LL COMB THE JUNGLES FOR *THOTH-AMON* MYSELF, WITHOUT *SORCERY!*

SOUTH... AYE, *SOUTH*... BEATING WINGS IN THE JUNGLE NIGHT... TO THE GREAT *WATERFALL*...

*HOLD*, MY ROYAL FRIEND! ANY MOMENT NOW...

...THEN *EAST*, TO THE *LAND OF NO RETURN*... TO THE GREAT *MOUNTAINS*... TO THE *GREAT STONE SKULL*, WHERE--*UNNNH!*

RIMUSH-- WHAT'S *WRONG*--?

THEN, IN A CLEARER, MORE NORMAL VOICE, THE OLD CONJURER GOES ON:

YOU WILL FIND THOTH-AMON AT THE *END OF THE WORLD*, WHERE THE *SERPENT-FOLK* RULED OF OLD--

-- ERE THE COMING-- OF MENNNN

*R'MUSH!*

WHAT THE DEVIL *HAPPENED* TO HIM, MBEGA?

HE CRUMPLED UP-- AS IF SUDDENLY STABBED BY A *KNIFE*.

NO KNIFE TOUCHED HIM, AQUILONIAN...

...BUT HE IS *DEAD*, ALL THE SAME!

AS IF STRUCK BY *LIGHTNING*-- OR AS IF BITTEN BY A DEADLY *SERPENT!*

124

SOON AFTERWARD...

HEAD OF NERGAL, SIRE-- I WON'T *HEAR* OF IT!

I'LL *NOT* HAVE YOU LARKING OFF INTO THE JUNGLES ALONE WITHOUT A COMPANY OF STOUT *AQUI-LONIANS* AT YOUR BACK!

PERHAPS I CAN'T MARCH WITH THIS ACCURSED LEG, BUT I CAN *RIDE*, AT LEAST...!

*NO*, PALLANTIDES! YOU, LIKE YOUR OWN SOLDIERS, ARE WASTED BY *WOUNDS* AND *FEVER*-- AND I CAN'T WAIT FOR YOU TO RECOVER.

*KING MBEGA* HAS OFFERED ME THE PICK OF HIS TROOPS...

BESIDES, IF I STAY HERE IN ZEMBABWEI MUCH LONGER, THOTH-AMON MAY HAVE CREPT BACK TO THE SAFETY OF HIS *STYGIAN LAIR*-- PERHAPS EVEN FLED TO VENDHYA OR KHITAI, OR THE *WORLD'S EDGE*, FOR ALL I KNOW!

THE OLD DEVIL HASN'T LOST *ALL* HIS MAGIC, EVEN IF WE DID DE-FEAT HIM AND HIS ALLIES. *

*LAST ISSUE. -- ROY.

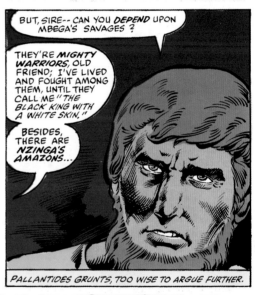

BUT, SIRE-- CAN YOU *DEPEND* UPON MBEGA'S *SAVAGES*?

THEY'RE *MIGHTY WARRIORS*, OLD FRIEND; I'VE LIVED AND FOUGHT AMONG THEM, UNTIL THEY CALL ME "*THE BLACK KING WITH A WHITE SKIN.*"

BESIDES, THERE ARE *NZINGA'S AMAZONS*...

PALLANTIDES GRUNTS, TOO WISE TO ARGUE FURTHER.

HE KNOWS THAT, MORE THAN TWENTY YEARS AGO, CONAN-- THEN A ZINGARAN BUCCANEER-- HAD VISITED THE COUNTRY OF THE BLACK QUEEN *NZINGA*.

THEY HAD SHARED THE MUTUAL RESPECT OF SWORN FOES... AND PASSIONATE WARRIORS.*

*SEE SAVAGE SWORD *41. --R.T.

AND NOW, JUST A WEEK PAST, A COMPANY OF BLACK AMAZONS HAD APPEARED IN ZEMBABWEI, TO REPRESENT THEIR QUEEN AT *MBEGA'S CORONATION*.

THEY WERE LED BY HER *DAUGHTER*-- ALSO CALLED *NZINGA*-- A LITHE LIONESS OF TWENTY RAINS.

THE AILING GENERAL CAN WELL IMAGINE THE YOUNGER NZINGA'S REACTION TO THE NEWS OF HIS MONARCH'S MISSION:

WE WILL GO WITH YOU, CONAN OF AQUILONIA!

HER FEATHER-TUFTED SPEAR AT HIS FEET-- SYMBOL OF HER OFFER OF ALLIANCE.

MY THANKS, NZINGA, DAUGHTER OF NZINGA.

THUS, PALLANTIDES TRIES ANOTHER TACK:

STILL, SIRE, IT MIGHT BE A THOUSAND LEAGUES TO THIS-- THIS LAND OF NO RETURN, OF WHICH A DEAD CONJURER SPOKE.

EVEN MBEGA HAS NO MAPS OF THAT REGION, YOU SAID.

MAPS ARE FOR MARCHING MEN, OLD FRIEND.

AND HOW WILL YOU GO? FLY?

THAT IS, PRINCE CONN AND I SHALL RIDE THEM-- AS SHALL THE PICK OF MBEGA'S ROYAL GUARD.

YES-- FLY! WE'LL BE RIDING THE WYVERNS-- THOSE FLYING DRAGONS TRAINED BY MBEGA'S DEAD TWIN, *

LUCKILY, WHEN THOTH-AMON ESCAPED ON ONE OF THE BRUTES, NOT ALL WERE LET LOOSE.

*LAST ISSUE. --ROY.

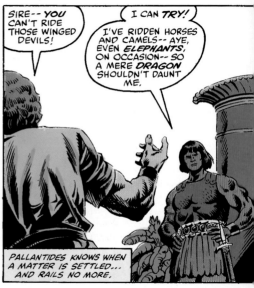

SIRE-- YOU CAN'T RIDE THOSE WINGED DEVILS!

I CAN TRY!

I'VE RIDDEN HORSES AND CAMELS-- AYE, EVEN ELEPHANTS, ON OCCASION-- SO A MERE DRAGON SHOULDN'T DAUNT ME.

PALLANTIDES KNOWS WHEN A MATTER IS SETTLED... AND RAILS NO MORE.

YET, THE CIMMERIAN-BORN SOVEREIGN SOON LEARNS THERE IS MUCH IN WHAT HIS GENERAL HAS SAID...

WELL, MBEGA-- SOME OF YOUR MEN HAVE MASTERED THESE THINGS, SURELY ENOUGH.

TIME FOR ME TO TRY-- THOUGH I'D PREFER NOT BEING TIED TO THE SADDLE, THIS WAY.

THOSE OF MY MEN WHO RIDE THE WYVERNS, DID SO ERE NOW, CONAN.

I WOULD NOT LOSE YOU, AFTER THE GOOD FRIEND YOU HAVE BEEN TO ME.

THEN, CONAN IS *ALOFT*--AND FEELING SENSATIONS WHICH EVEN HE HAS SELDOM KNOWN BEFORE--

--THOUGH THE GOOD WIZARD *PELIAS* DID SEND HIM WINGING IT ON A *SIMILAR* CREATURE, TO HIS EPIC BATTLE WITH *TSOTHA-LANTI*, YEARS AGO.

HE IS WRAPPED THUS IN REVERIE WHEN, FAR BELOW, A *GAZELLE* SUDDENLY BOLTS FROM COVER--

--AND HE IS SUDDENLY *GLAD* TO BE STRAPPED TO THE WYVERN'S BACK.

*WHOA, YOU HAIRY DEVIL!*

*UP, I SAY! UP!*

*HAH!* AT LEAST YOU RESPOND TO A *SPEAR-BLOW* THE WAY MBEGA SAID YOU WOULD...

...AND MY STOMACH CAN RETURN TO ITS NORMAL PLACE IN MY INSIDES.

FRANKLY, IF I HAD A CHOICE, I'D TAKE MY CHANCES *AFOOT* WITH THE WARRIORS OF NZINGA AND MBEGA.

*BESIDES*-- YOU *SMELL!*

STILL, WHEN THE WAR-EXPEDITION SETS OUT, DAYS LATER, THERE IS NO DENYING THAT THE WYVERNS MOVE AT A SPEED WHICH FAR OUTSTRIPS THOSE ON THE GROUND...

*HO, FATHER! LOOK AT ME!*

*HOLD THE REINS, BOY!*

BUT CONAN SMILES TO HIMSELF TO NOTE THAT HIS *SON AND HEIR-APPARENT* IS AMONG THE BEST OF ALL THE DRAGON-RIDERS.

BELOW, LIKE A COLUMN OF BLACK ANTS WHEN THEY CAN BE SEEN AT ALL THROUGH THE THICK FOLIAGE, MBEGA'S WARRIORS MARCH UNDER ORDERS OF COUNT TROCERO, AT A SPEED WHICH EVEN CONAN'S TOUGH AQUILONIAN VETERANS WOULD BE HARD-PUT TO MATCH.

TROCERO HIMSELF, UNABLE BY REASON OF AGE TO KEEP UP, IS OFTEN BORNE ON A LITTER BY STALWART WARRIORS--THOUGH HE WALKS PROUDLY, WHENEVER HE CAN.

BEHIND THE MEN, AND SEPARATED FROM THEM BY A TRAIN OF MEN AND WOMEN BEARING FOOD AND SUPPLIES, COME YOUNG NZINGA AND HER TIRELESS BLACK AMAZONS...

...AND CONAN MUSES, FROM ABOVE, THAT HE'D HAVE BEEN HONORED TO HAVE SUCH A WOMAN AS THIS NZINGA FOR HIS DAUGHTER.

BY DAY, CONAN AND HIS SCOUTING FORCE RANGE FAR AHEAD, SPYING OUT THE BEST ROUTES IN THIS HORSELESS LAND.

BY NIGHT, HE RETURNS TO TROCERO AND NZINGA, FOR HE KNOWS THAT BOTH AIR AND GROUND FORCES MUST STRIKE AS ONE, IF THEY ARE TO OVERCOME BOTH THE SUPREME WIZARDRY OF THOTH-AMON...

...AND WHATEVER GRIM, DESPERATE ALLIES, HE MAY FIND IN THE LEGENDARY LAND OF NO RETURN.

IT HAS BEEN **TWO MONTHS** SINCE MEN AND BEASTS LEFT ZEMBABWEI'S GATES-- AND THE HAZE-REDDENED SUN IS SINKING TOWARD THE JAGGED HORIZON-- WHEN THE CIMMERIAN SIGHTS HIS FIRST *LANDMARK:*

THE *GREAT WATERFALL,* A WHITE GLITTER THAT PLUNGES FROM TOWERING CLIFFS.

FOR A MOMENT, HE PONDERS WHETHER HE OUGHT TO RETURN TO THE GROUND FORCE, NOW FAR BEHIND...

BUT **NO!** HE'LL MAKE A FEW CASTS *EAST-WARD,* AS DEAD RIMUSH SAID, AND THEN SWING **NORTH** AGAIN.

PLENTY OF TIME TO RE-JOIN HIS TROOPS BE-FORE NIGHT-FALL.

COME, LADS!

AND **PRINCE CONN,** GRINNING ACROSS THE INTERVENING DIS-TANCE, FOLLOWS HIS **LEAD** -- JUST AS MBEGA'S WARRIORS, IN TURN, FOLLOW **HIM.**

MOVE, OLD SCALE-BACK!

A *KING,* CALLS!

THE LAD HAS BEEN THROUGH **MUCH** SINCE HE JOINED HIS SIRE'S EXPEDITION AT NEBTHU, ON THE RIVER STYX-- AND HAS SURELY LEARNED A FEW THINGS ABOUT BEING A WARRI-OR-KING, CONAN MUSES.

HIS SIRE DECIDES HE WAS **RIGHT** TO IGNORE HIS COUNCILORS' ADVICE AND BRING HIS SON ALONG ON EVEN SUCH A DANGEROUS MISSION.

IT IS LATE AFTERNOON--NIGH TIME FOR *TURNING BACK* -- WHEN CONAN SEES HIS SON SUDDENLY **POINT...**

THERE, FATHER! THERE!

BY CROM!

THE GREAT STONE SKULL!

AS HE BEHOLDS THAT MOUNTAIN OF CHALK-WHITE STONE INTO WHICH AN IMMENSE, GRINNING *DEATH'S HEAD* HAS BEEN CARVED, CONAN'S BARBARIAN HERITAGE OF *SUPER-STITION* WHELMS UP WITHIN HIM IN THE GLOOM.

BUT, HE HAS LITTLE CHANCE TO COME TO GRIPS WITH THOSE EERIE PREMONITIONS-- FOR, AT THAT VERY MOMENT--

--TERROR STRIKES!

ARRRHH--!

A SUDDEN SHOCK RUNS THROUGH HIS BURLY FRAME-- LEAVING HIM GASPING, HIS SENSES ASWIM--

--AS THE *WYVERN*, AFFECTED BY THE SAME WEIRD FORCE, HURTLES TOWARD THE HAUNTED, SHADOWY PLAIN BELOW!

WITH A HEAVE THAT WOULD BREAK A HORSE'S JAW, CONAN *JERKS BACK* THE DRAGON'S REINS--

WHOA!

WHOA, YOU SLIMY--!

THE WYVERN RESPONDS SLUGGISHLY--

YET, RESPOND IT *DOES*, OPENING RIBBED WINGS TO CATCH THE RUSHING WIND--

--*TOO LATE* TO DO MORE THAN *SLOW* ITS HEADLONG FALL--

--WITH CONAN TUMBLING PELL-MELL FROM ITS BACK, AMID A SKELTER OF ROCKS AND EARTH!

⸘UNNGNN!⸘

EVEN AS HE STRIVES TO CLEAR HIS GROGGY WITS, THE BARBARIAN-KING WONDERS IF THE WYVERN FLEW THROUGH SOME UPDRAFT OF *NOXIOUS GAS.*

AND, IF IT *DID*, THEN WHAT OF--

CONN--?

FOR THE LOVE OF MITRA!

CONN!

ONE BY ONE, THE STUNNED DRAGONS PLUMMET FROM THE SKY-- BUT THE RUSH OF AIR SEEMS TO *ROUSE* THE FAINTING LAD--

--SO THAT HE JERKS BACK THE *REINS,* WITH EVERY OUNCE OF VIGOR IN HIS LITHE YOUNG THEWS--

STOP, CURSE YOUR HIDE!

--AND HIS WYVERN LURCHES DRUNKENLY-- BUT MORE OR LESS SAFELY-- TO THE GROUND.

CONN! CONN MY SON--

ARE YOU *ALL RIGHT,* BOY?

I-- STRUCK MY HEAD-- ON A *ROCK,* I THINK--

BUT, WE CIMMERIANS ARE TOO *HARD-HEADED* TO KILL THAT WAY, EH, FATHER?

AYE, LAD,

AYE!

TWO OF THE WARRIORS OF MBEGA, ALAS, ARE LESS FORTUNATE.

AAAAAA

FAILING TO RECOVER FROM THE EFFECTS OF THE WIZARDLY SKY BARRIER, THEY *CRASH TO EARTH* WITH A SICKENING CRUNCH OF SNAPPING BONES.

THE REST, HOWEVER, MANAGE SOMEHOW TO BRING THEIR NUMBED REPTILE MOUNTS FLOUNDERING TO THE GROUND...

...THOUGH SOMETIMES WITH MARROW-SHAKING IMPACT.

THEN, AS THE BLACK WARRIORS, RECOVERING FROM THEIR DIZZINESS, WORK AT HOBBLING THEIR BEASTS...

FATHER-- *LOOK THERE!*

WHAT IS IT, LAD? IF IT'S THAT GRINNING *SKULL OF STONE,* I'VE ALREADY SEEN--

IT-- *ISN'T* THAT, SIRE...

THEN WHAT *IS* IT, LAD, AMID THIS *DEAD PLAIN,* THAT INTERESTS YOU SO?

SURELY, YOU'VE SEEN ENOUGH *ROCKS* EVEN IN YOUR BRIEF LIFE-TIME TO--

THEN, KING CONAN STOPS SHORT...

FOR, HE SUDDENLY BEHOLDS THAT WHICH HAD BEEN, BUT MOMENTS BEFORE, *WHOLLY INVISIBLE* TO THE NAKED EYE FROM ABOVE--

--AND HE SEES THAT THE *CLIFF,* WHICH FROM THE AIR HAD SEEMED A CARVED SKULL, NOW APPEARS AS THE FACADE OF A *SPLENDID, ORNATE PALACE!*

CROM'S THUNDER!

WHICH OF THE TWO SIGHTS IS *REAL,* I WONDER--

--THE *BARREN LANDSCAPE* WE VIEWED FROM THE SKY--

--OR THIS MEADOW, WITH ITS SPANGLE OF *FLOWERS*?

FATHER--THE *AIR*--!

YOU'RE RIGHT, SON-- THAT'S THE TRUE TEST.

AND IT SMELLS OF *PER-FUMED FLOWERS* AND *LUSH GRASSES*.

WAS IT SOME *HYPNOTIC VAPOR* WE SOARED THROUGH, THEN, THAT--?

*ANGALIA!*

EH? WHAT IS IT, MKWAWA?

THE *PALACE,* KING CONAN!

SOMEONE COMES!

AND INDEED, FIGURES ARE DRIFTING THROUGH THE PILLARS, DOWN THE SMOOTH STAIRS, COMING TOWARD THEM THROUGH THE SWAYING GRASS:

WOMEN ALL-- DUSKY, SINUOUS, WITH SMILING RED LIPS AND EYES LIKE BLACK JEWELS.

LITTLE CRYSTAL BELLS ARE WOVEN THROUGH THE COILS OF THEIR JET-DARK HAIR, SO THAT EACH FIGURE IS SURROUNDED BY A FAINTLY CHIMING *MUSIC.*

WHAT SHALL WE DO, KING CONAN?

PERHAPS WE CAN *LEARN* SOMETHING FROM THESE WOMEN, WHO DO NOT *SEEM* DANGEROUS.

BESIDES, THE GROGGY DRAGONS COULD USE A *REST*.

HALF OF YOU, COME WITH ME; THE OTHERS WILL GUARD THE WYVERNS.

AND MKWAWA-- DETAIL ONE MAN TO FLY BACK TO THE *ARMY*, TO SET THEM ON OUR TRAIL.

STILL, AS HE WALKS BOLDLY FORWARD, CONAN MUSES THAT THERE IS SOMETHING *WRONG* WITH A PLACE THAT CHANGES ITS ENTIRE APPEARANCE IN THE SPACE OF A FEW HEARTBEATS.

*Three nights later:*

ON THE MARBLE FLOOR OF A GREAT HALL, CONAN AND HIS MEN SPRAWL ON NESTS OF SILKEN CUSHIONS, FEELING CURIOUSLY LAZY AND RELAXED... THEIR BELLIES FILLED WITH SUBTLY FLAVORED VIANDS...

...AND ONLY YOUNG *CONN* SEEMS TO EVINCE MORE THAN A PASSING INTEREST IN THE SENSUOUSLY DANCING *WOMEN* NEARBY.

135

HE HIMSELF HAD NOT BEEN MUCH OLDER, CONAN MUSES, WHEN HE HAD MET *URSLA, THE BEAR-WOMAN*, PRIESTESS OF THE MOUNTAIN FASTNESS. *

AFTER THAT TIMELY ENCOUNTER, HE HAD SOON BEGUN HIS ROAMINGS, AND QUICKLY SHED THE GRIM PURITANISM OF A CIMMERIAN VILLAGE.

SO, QUEEN LILIT...

...YOU SAY THIS CAVE-CITY OF YOURS IS CALLED *YANYOGA?*

*SEE CONAN THE BARBARIAN #48. --ROY.

YES, CONAN. AND I AM TRULY SORRY I CANNOT HELP YOU.

BUT, I FEAR I KNOW NOTHING OF THIS *THOTH-AMON* YOU SEEK... NOR WERE WE AWARE THAT THESE CLIFFS LOOK *SKULL-LIKE* FROM THE SKY.

FEW PEOPLE *COME* TO US THAT WAY, OF COURSE.

OF COURSE.

BUT I'M STILL CURIOUS HOW A *CITY OF WOMEN* CAME TO BE HERE... IF YOU *KNOW.*

OH, WE KNOW WELL ENOUGH, MY LORD...

"A FEW CENTURIES AGO, A MIGHTY *KING* IN DISTANT VENDHYA SENT FORTH A FLEET ON A TRADING MISSION TO IRANISTAN.

"A *TYPHOON* BLEW THIS FLEET FAR OFF ITS COURSE ACROSS THE *SOUTHERN OCEAN...*

"...AND THE BATTERED *SURVIVORS* MADE LANDFALL NOT MANY LEAGUES FROM HERE.

"THEY FOUND, AND EN-SLAVED, A RACE OF SMALL, YELLOW-SKINNED *ABORIGINES,* WHO STILL SERVE US AS *SERFS.*

136

THE VENDHYANS THEMSELVES MATED WITH *SLAVE GIRLS* WHO HAD BEEN PART OF THEIR CARGO.

THESE FOLK, AND THEIR DESCENDANTS, CARVED YANYOGA OUT OF THE SOFT, CHALKY ROCK OF THIS CLIFF FACE.

INTERESTING.

THIS PALACE, CONAN THINKS, IS REALLY TOO *OSTENTATIOUS* FOR HIS TASTES...

...OR IS IT JUST THAT *WINE* HAS DULLED HIS WOLF-SHARP SENSES?

MEANWHILE, IF ONLY WITH HIS EYES THUS FAR, PRINCE CONN IS DEFINITELY PROVING HIMSELF HIS FATHER'S SON...

AND AS THE DANCE ENDS, HE OBSERVES HOW THE GIRL *LINGERS*, LOOKING BACK AT HIM FROM THE SHADOW OF A DISTANT PILLAR.

IT'S NOW OR NEVER, CONN KNOWS...

...SO IT MIGHT AS WELL BE *NOW*.

NOW WHERE THE DEVIL DID--

OH, *THERE* YOU ARE!

AND WHERE ELSE SHOULD I BE, YOUNG PRINCE?

YOU'RE VERY *BEAUTIFUL!* I--

NOT HERE! THE *QUEEN--!*

*WHERE,* THEN?

COME...!

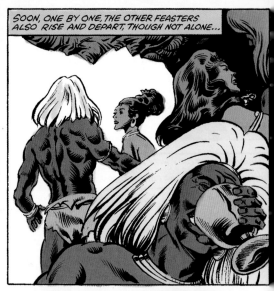

SOON, ONE BY ONE, THE OTHER FEASTERS ALSO RISE AND DEPART, THOUGH NOT ALONE...

...LEAVING THEIR KING DOZING ON HIS CUSHIONS, AS HIS HONEY WINE MAKES A PUDDLE ON THE MARBLE FLOOR.

NOW, SWARTHY *SERVING-MEN* APPEAR IN THE NEARLY EMPTY HALL, GLIDING AMONG THE SEATS ABANDONED BY CONAN'S GUARDSMEN.

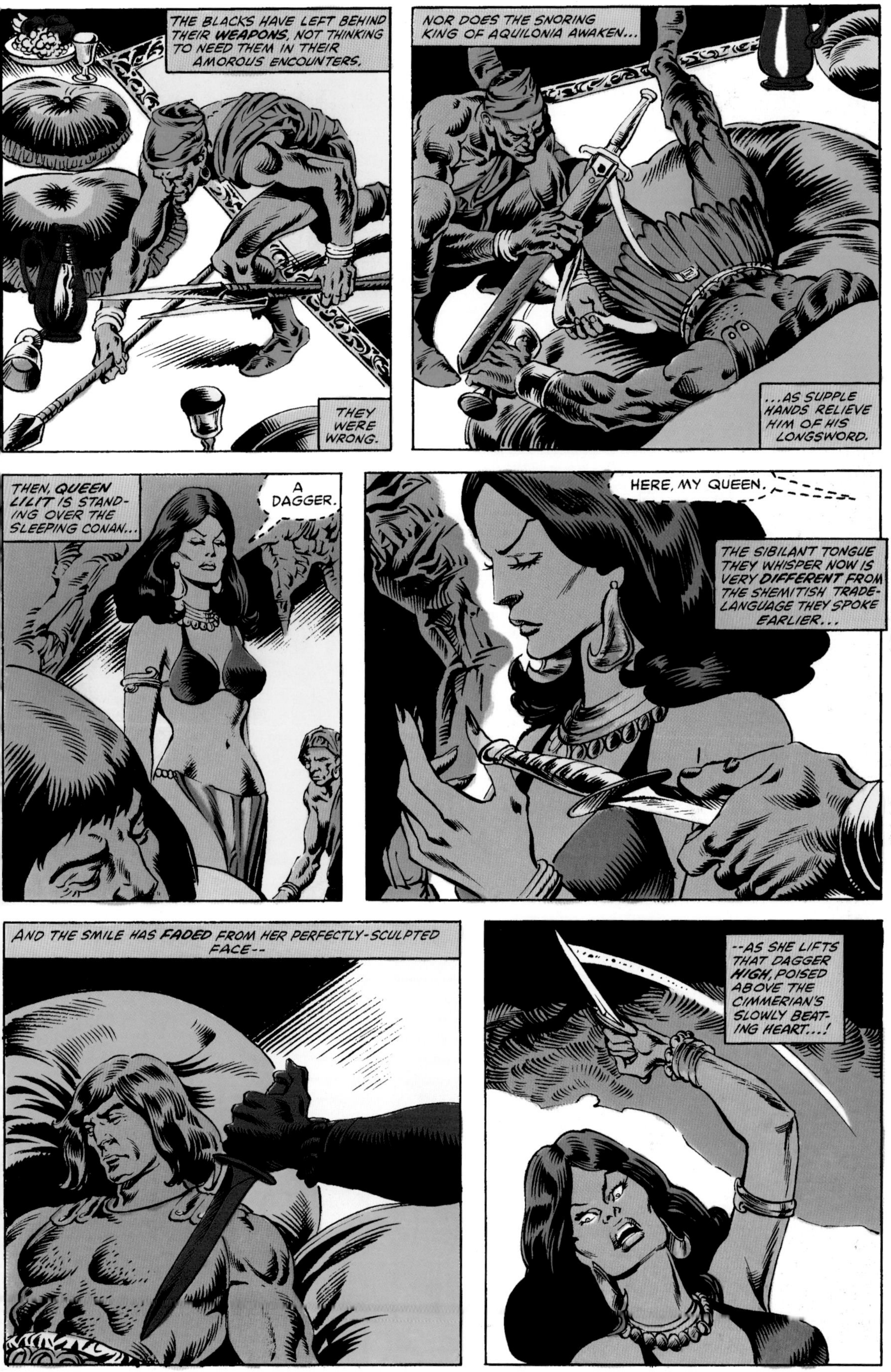
THE BLACKS HAVE LEFT BEHIND THEIR WEAPONS, NOT THINKING TO NEED THEM IN THEIR AMOROUS ENCOUNTERS.
THEY WERE WRONG.
NOR DOES THE SNORING KING OF AQUILONIA AWAKEN...
...AS SUPPLE HANDS RELIEVE HIM OF HIS LONGSWORD.
THEN, QUEEN LILIT IS STANDING OVER THE SLEEPING CONAN...
A DAGGER.
HERE, MY QUEEN.
THE SIBILANT TONGUE THEY WHISPER NOW IS VERY DIFFERENT FROM THE SHEMITISH TRADE-LANGUAGE THEY SPOKE EARLIER...
AND THE SMILE HAS FADED FROM HER PERFECTLY-SCULPTED FACE--
--AS SHE LIFTS THAT DAGGER HIGH, POISED ABOVE THE CIMMERIAN'S SLOWLY BEATING HEART...!

YOU'RE...SO VERY *LOVELY*. I WANT...

YOUR SWORD, MY LORD.... IT HURTS ME...!

WE, UH, CAN'T HAVE *THAT* NOW, CAN WE?

WELL, THAT'S EASILY TAKEN CARE OF.

I'LL JUST SET IT OVER BY THIS *COPPER CHEST*, AND--

NO! NO!!

WHAT IS WRONG, YOUNG PRINCE?

YOUR *REFLECTION*!

Y-YOUR *HEAD*!

YOU'RE ONE OF THE *SNAKE-PEOPLE* MY FATHER TOLD ME ABOUT!

THIS IS ALL A *TRAP*!

NO, MY LORD... I *SWEAR* IT...

140

YOU ARE *WRONG!* I AM ONLY A AAAAAAAAAAHH

EVEN AS HE DRIVES HIS GLEAMING BLADE HOME, YOUNG CONN IS SEIZED BY A HORRIBLE FEAR THAT HE HAS MADE A TRAGIC *MISTAKE...*

...BUT OF COURSE, HE HAS NOT.

AND, AS THE SERPENT-THING'S LIFE EBBS, AND DULL GRAY SCALES TAKE THE PLACE OF WARM DUSKY SKIN...

...AQUILONIA'S PRINCE IS SUDDENLY SICK.

UNNNHNN~-!

WHEN IT IS OVER, HE FEELS WEAK, BUT PURGED,...HIS MIND CLEAR.

CONN KNOWS THE ANCIENT MYTHS OF THE *SERPENT-FOLK,* SLAIN IN LEGEND BY *MIRA THE LIGHT-BRINGER...*

...BUT IN ACTUALITY BY *KULL,* HERO-KING OF ANCIENT VALUSIA.

ONCE, LONG BEFORE EVEN KULL'S TIME, THEY HAD *RULED* OVER ORDINARY MEN... AND THEY COULD CLOUD MEN'S MINDS TO PASS AMONG THEM, BUT THEY COULD NOT FOOL *MIRRORS.*

NOW, THE *LAST SURVIVORS* OF THIS LOATHSOME RACE HAVE FLED TO THE *WORLD'S RIM* TO BIDE THEIR TIME...

...AND IT MAY BE THAT ONLY *CONN* KNOWS THEIR HORRIBLE SECRET!

FATHER...!

AS, ELSEWHERE--

LILIT! HOLD!

WHO DARES--?

YOU! WHO COMMANDS HERE, STYGIAN-- YOU OR I?

VENGEANCE IS MINE, LILIT.

IN ALL ELSE, I YIELD TO YOU....BUT IN THIS I AM ADAMANT.

THE CIMMERIAN IS THOTH-AMON'S CAPTIVE!

MY CENTURIES WEIGH HEAVILY UPON ME NOW, SINCE THAT BARBARIAN DOG SMASHED FIRST THE BLACK RING AT NEBTHU...

...THEN NENAUNIR IN ZEMBABWEI.

I KNOW YOUR CUNNING HEART, HUMAN JACKAL!

YOU THINK TO SACRIFICE HIM TO FATHER SET, GOD OF US SERPENT-FOLK....AND THUS REGAIN YOUR FAVORED POSITION.

BUT, THOUGH MY FORM NOW BE OLD, SHRUNKEN AND FRAIL....MY MAGIC STILL IS SUFFICIENT TO DESTROY HIM.

BUT I, TOO, HAVE PLANS FOR THE CIMMERIAN...

...AND IT IS THOSE PLANS THAT SHALL--

URRKK

BY MAMAJAMBO'S WAR CLUB!

WE HAVE COME JUST IN TIME!

COME, WARRIORS!

LESS HALE AND HEARTY THAN YOU I MAY BE, BUT I MUST SEE HOW MY *KING* FARE IN THIS ACCURSED--

BY ALL THE GODS-- *THOTH-AMON!*

OH, AYE? WE DRAW NEAR A *SKULL-CLIFF* THAT BECOMES A MEADOW-GIRT PALACE...

...TO FIND THE LORD CONAN *SNORING* LIKE A BESOTTED DRUNKARD...

...AND THIS *WOMAN-THING* BENDING OVER HIM WITH A KNIFE, AS WELL AS AN *OLD MAN IN A ROBE!*

WHAT MONSTROUS SORCERY *IS* THIS, ANYWAY?

THE...SNAKE... THAT... SPEAKS!

THE SNAKE THAT SPEAKS!

OLD MAN, YOU SPEAK OF THAT WHICH *NONE* SHOULD NAME ALOUD!

CAN IT BE, THOUGH, THAT THE OLD MYTHS ARE *TRUE*?

THE PROOF OF IT LIES *DEAD* AT YOUR FEET, NZINGA.

LOOK! EVEN AS WE FENCE WITH WORDS--

--IT *CHANGES*, IT'S REPTILE BODY LOSING ALL HUMAN SEMBLANCE, MOMENT BY MOMENT! IT--

TROCERO! NZINGA! BEWARE!--

THE SERPENT-MEN!

OLD MAN-- IT APPEARS YOU MAY HAVE BEEN *RIGHT*, AFTER ALL.

PRINCESS-- YOU ARE A MASTER OF UNDER-STATEMENT!

YOUR MOTHER, THE QUEEN, SHOULD MAKE YOU CHIEF AMONG HER *DIPLOMATS*!

THEN, BOTH TROCERO AND NZINGA ARE FAR TOO BUSY FOR FURTHER SPEECH...

--AS WARRIORS AND THE HISSING HORDE FALL UPON EACH OTHER!

AND, IN THE MAD CLASH THAT FOLLOWS, NEITHER OF THEM NOTICES THE STRANGEST, MOST *INEXPLI-CABLE* THING OF ALL:

BOTH THE SPRAWLING, UNCONSCIOUS *CIMMERIAN* AND HIS SORCEROUS ARCH-FOE *THOTH-AMON* HAVE VANISHED AS IF MELTED INTO THIN AIR!

NEARLY TWO DECADES OF KINGSHIP OVER A CULTURED REALM HAVE LAID BUT A THIN VENEER OF CIVILIZATION OVER CONAN'S PRIMITIVE SOUL.

THUS, AS HE WAKES FROM HIS *DRUGGED SLUMBER*, THE CIMMERIAN'S SENSES ARE INSTANTLY *SHARP...*

UNNNHH--!

AND HIS EARS DETECT THE DULL BOOM OF *WAVES* POUNDING A ROCKY SHORE, EVEN AS HIS NOSTRILS TASTE THE *SALT TANG* IN THE AIR.

FROM A BRIEF GLANCE AT *STARRY SKIES* AS HE STARTS TO RISE, HE KNOWS THAT THE NEARBY SEA STRETCHES AWAY TO THE *SOUTH.*

BUT, AS FAR AS HIS SMOLDERING GAZE CAN PENETRATE THE MURK OF NIGHT, HE CAN SEE *NO LAND.*

IT IS AS IF HE LIES AT THE *WORLD'S VERY EDGE,* AND THE SHORE THEREOF IS WASHED BY THE ENDLESS SEAS OF *ETERNITY.*

HOW, HE WONDERS, DID HE *COME* HERE?

HE DOES NOT WONDER FOR LONG.

WE MEET *AGAIN,* DOG OF CIMMERIA!

FOR THE *LAST* TIME, JACKAL OF STYGIA!

WARY OF THOTH-AMON'S REMAINING POWERS, HOWEVER, HE MAKES NO MOVE TOWARD THE GAUNT WIZARD.

YOU PONDER, I KNOW, WHY I BROUGHT YOU HERE *ALIVE* WITH THE AID OF THE UNSEEN *DEMONS* WHO STILL SERVE ME.

YOU HAVE HOUNDED ME DOWN THE *LENGTH OF THE WORLD,* BARBARIAN...

ONE BY ONE, YOU HAVE *SUNDERED* FROM ME MY MOST POWERFUL ALLIES;

THE *WHITE HAND* IN WINTRY HYPERBOREA... THE *BLACK RING* AT NEBTHU...EVEN *NENAUNIR* IN ZEMBABWEI.

NOW, THERE IS *NO FURTHER* REALM TO WHICH I CAN FLY FOR *REFUGE.*

HERE AT THE WORLD'S EDGE DWELL THE *LAST* OF THE ANCIENT SERPENT-FOLK, WHO RULED THE EARTH BEFORE THE COMING OF MEN.

NOR HAVE THEY EVER RELINQUISHED THEIR HOPE OF *REGAINING* THEIR POWER ON THIS PITIFUL PLANET.

FROM THEM, I GAINED THE KNOWLEDGE THAT ENABLED ME TO BECOME THE *EMISSARY OF SET,* THE SERPENT-GOD.

AT THE SAME TIME, I HELD THEM IN *CHECK*-- HAVING NO WISH TO SHARE MY OWN RULE WITH THE *CHILDREN OF THE SNAKE.*

MY SPLENDID PLANS *YOU ALONE* HAVE THWARTED-- *HOW,* I KNOW NOT!

YOU ARE NO PRIEST OR PROPHET OR WIZARD-- ONLY A CRUDE, IGNORANT *ADVENTURER,* FOR THE MOMENT TOSSED HIGH BY THE WAVES OF FATE.

PERHAPS YOUR DEGENERATE *WESTERN GODS* HAVE HELPED YOU IN SUBTLE WAYS NEITHER OF US KNOWS.

BUT, ALL IS NOT YET *LOST!*

FOR, UNTO *SET* HIMSELF I SHALL OFFER UP YOUR *SOUL* IN SACRIFICE, AND THE SLITHERING GOD SHALL *FEAST WELL* ON IT.

THEN, RESTORED TO FAVOR, I SHALL UNLEASH THE UNCANNY POWERS OF THE SERPENT-FOLK IN *ONE LAST, GREAT CRUSADE--!*

*THEN, SUDDENLY, CONAN STRIKES FROM SILENCE--!*

YOU'VE DONE *ENOUGH* TALKING, SORCERER-- FOR NOW, OR FOR A DOZEN LIFETIMES.

*TONIGHT,* BY KING CONAN'S HAND--

--YOU **DIE!**

RRGK

CONAN'S TIGERISH CHARGE HAS TAKEN THE STRANGELY EMACIATED STYGIAN BY SURPRISE...

...AND ITS **IMPACT** HURLS THE PAIR BEYOND THE BOULDER, TO FALL LOCKED TOGETHER UPON DAMP SANDS.

YET, THOUGH LITTLE STRENGTH REMAINS IN THOTH-AMON'S WITHERED FORM, HIS WIZARDLY POWERS STILL LEND HIM **UNEARTHLY SOURCES**--

AND, EVEN AS KING CONAN'S FINGERS **LOCK** ON THAT DUSKY, FRAGILE NECK...

...A TOUCH LIKE **FREEZING FIRE** BRUSHES LIGHTLY AGAINST HIS BROW--

AAARRRR

--AND **COLD WAVES OF BLACKNESS** ENGULF HIS CONSCIOUSNESS.

IT SEEMS TO THE BARBARIAN THAT HE SINKS THROUGH **DARKLING WATERS** WHOSE BITE BE-NUMB HIS FLESH...

147

...UNTIL HIS *NAKED SPIRIT* ALONE WRITHES THERE ON THE SANDS.

BUT, STILL IS *THOTH-AMON* HELD HELPLESS IN CONAN'S GRIP-- FOR, IT IS AS IF THE SORCERER, TOO, HAS LEFT HIS FLESHLY SHELL BEHIND--

-- AND *TWO IM-PALPABLE SPIRITS,* LOCKED IN CONFLICT, RISE FROM THE VORTEX INTO A DIM REGION BEYOND THE WORLD!

ABOUT THEM, *MIST* SWIRLS AND BILLOWS, GRAY AND COLORLESS.

ABOVE THEM, *BLACK STARS* BURN AGAINST NATURAL SKIES; THE LIGHT FROM THEM IS AS COLD AS THE BREATH OF ARCTIC WINDS.

CONAN FIGHTS AS *NEVER BEFORE*--

--NOT TRULY WITH HIS *MASSIVE THEWS*, BUT AS IF WITH THE VERY ESSENCE OF *COURAGE* AND *MANHOOD* THAT BURNS IN HIS HEART.

AND, IN SPIRIT FORM, *THOTH-AMON*, TOO, HAS STRENGTH FAR BEYOND WHAT HIS HUMAN PHYSIQUE EVER POSSESSED.

THEN, SUDDENLY, THE WIZARD *SHRIEKS SOUND-LESSLY*-- AN AWFUL, HOLLOW CRY OF AGONY AND DESPAIR--

--AND THE COIL OF *WRITHING VAPOR* WHICH HAD BEEN THOTH-AMON'S SPIRIT *MELTS* IN THE CIMMERIAN'S GRASP--

--*DISINTEGRATING* AND FADING INTO THE *COLD MISTS* OF THE VOID.

CONAN FLOATS FOR A TIME...PANTING, WHILE STRENGTH SEEPS BACK INTO HIS EXHAUSTED SPIRIT.

SOMEHOW HE KNOWS THAT THE LIFE FORCE OF THOTH-AMON... NO LONGER EXISTS.

AFTER A WHILE, HE COMES TO HIMSELF ON THE SANDY SHORE BY THAT NAMELESS SEA.

A *WEEPING BOY* CLINGS TO HIM...

DON'T DIE, FATHER... DON'T DIE...PLEASE...

I'M ...ALIVE, LAD...

...BUT WHAT OF...THOTH-AMON?

FATHER! THANK CROM AND MITRA!

I--I STABBED HIM, FATHER! I STABBED HIM MANY TIMES--!

THEN, CONAN LOOKS BEYOND HIS SON AT WHAT THE BOY HAD USED, THEN FLUNG ASIDE:

THE SWORD HE HIMSELF GAVE TO CONN ON HIS LAST BIRTHDAY.

I REMEMBER NOW! THE OLD WHITE DRUID DIVIATIX SCRATCHED A SIGN ON IT--

--THE SIGN OF PROTECTION... THE LOOPED CROSS OF MITRA, LORD OF LIGHT...

THE CROSS OF LIFE!

I--I DIDN'T KNOW WHAT TO DO, FATHER! HE WAS KILLING YOU, SO I--

YOU DID WELL, MY SON.

I YET LIVE, THOUGH CROM KNOWS I WAS CLOSE TO THE BLACK GATES OF DEATH.

BUT, THOSE GATES HAVE OPENED TO SWALLOW ANOTHER'S SOUL, NOT MINE.

LOOK!

WHAT--?

THEN, AS THEY GAZE AT THE DEAD MAN SPRAWLED ON THE SANDS...

...THE YEARS AT LAST TAKE THEIR VENGEANCE ON THE REMAINS OF THE MIGHTIEST MAGICIAN OF SHADOW-HAUNTED STYGIA...

...AS THEY MUST, ONE DAY...

...ON US ALL.

SHALL WE GO *WITHIN* NOW, FATHER-- TO FIGHT ALONGSIDE THE OTHERS?

IN A MOMENT, SON, AS SOON AS I FIND--

AH, *HERE* IT IS.

THOTH-AMON'S *RING!*

WHO *KNOWS* WHAT VILE SORCERY STILL LURKS WITHIN ITS SPARKLING DEPTHS?

WILL YOU TAKE IT BACK TO *TARANTIA,* SIRE?

NO, SON, IT WOULD BE *TOO TEMPTING* A PRIZE FOR MEN OF EVIL PURPOSE, OR EVEN FOR--

SO END *ALL* MAGICAL MUMMERY!

MAY IT *STAY* AT THE BOTTOM OF THE SEA FOR A *HUNDRED THOUSAND YEARS!*

NOW, HOW CAME YOU *HERE* IN TIME TO SAVE YOUR OLD FATHER, CONN.

I WAS...WITH A *GIRL,* WHO TURNED INTO A SNAKE-HEADED MONSTER, SO THAT I HAD TO SLAY HER.

JUST AS I WAS COMING BACK TO YOU, THE *AMAZONS* CAME IN, TO SLAY THE *QUEEN.*

*SHE* TURNED INTO A SNAKE-THING TOO, OF COURSE...

"THEN, THERE WAS *FIGHTING* EVERYWHERE-- SERPENT-MEN AGAINST OUR WARRIORS--

"...AND I COULDN'T REACH YOUR SIDE, THROUGH THE FRAY.

"BUT I SAW *THOTH-AMON* CARRY YOU FROM THE HALL...

"...AS IF HIS *MAGIC* GAVE HIM A SHORT SURGE OF STRENGTH.

"NO ONE SEEMED TO BE ABLE TO *SEE* THIS EXCEPT ME...AS IF A *SPELL* HID HIS ACTIONS.

151

"THERE WAS A *LONG BLACK TUNNEL* BEHIND THE TAPESTRY-- AND I FOLLOWED AS BEST I COULD..."

"YET, WHEN I GOT OUTSIDE UNDER THE STARS, THERE WERE SUCH HUGE *ROCKS*-- I COULDN'T TELL WHERE YOU WERE.

"SO I HAD TO SEARCH, AND *SEARCH*--

"THEN, AT LAST, I *FOUND* YOU-- FIGHTING THOTH-AMON UPON THE SANDS--

"AND IT WAS AS IF YOU WERE *ASLEEP*-- AS IF YOU WERE *FIGHTING* IN YOUR SLEEP--

"--AND THE STYGIAN WAS *ABOVE* YOU, POISED TO STRIKE THE FINAL BLOW--"

"--WHEN I *PREVENTED* HIM.

PRAISE MITRA I STRUCK IN *TIME!*

AS YOU YOURSELF SAID, LAD-- PRAISE *CROM* AND MITRA.

THOTH-AMON WAS THE *GREATEST* OF ALL THE FOES I'VE OVERCOME, AS MAN *OR* KING.

I'LL *MISS* THE OLD SCOUNDREL, IN A WAY...

...BUT NOT *TOO* MUCH.

I TAKE IT *THAT'S* THE WAY WE CAME?

AYE! WE'D BEST *HURRY*, IF WE'RE GOING TO JOIN THE FRAY BEFORE THE SERPENT-MEN ARE ALL *DEAD*.

I'LL BE GLAD WHEN THE *LAST* OF THEM IS DEAD, NO MATTER BY *WHOSE* HAND. STILL...

*HMMM*... DO YOU STILL HAVE YOUR *SWORD*, BOY?

YES, SIRE.

THEN, LET *ME* FIND AN APPROPRIATE MOPPING-UP WEAPON, AND WE'LL--

AH! *THERE'S* A COUPLE OF WHAT I'M AFTER!

COME ON! NOW THAT I THINK OF IT, I *DO* HUNGER TO SMASH IN THE HEADS OF A FEW SNAKE-MEN.

OH, AND BY THE WAY...

...*THANKS* FOR PUTTING A SWORD THROUGH OLD *THOTH-AMON* WHEN YOU DID...*SON*.

IT WAS MY PLEASURE... *FATHER*.

153

NEXT ISSUE: **CONAN THE AVENGER!**

75¢ 5 MAR 02480

MIGHTIEST MONARCH OF A TIME-LOST LAND!

# KING CONAN

FOR THE RING OF RAKHAMON, AND THE LIFE OF HIS QUEEN, CONAN MUST BATTLE—

--THE SORCERER IN THE REALM OF MADNESS!

# KING CONAN

Featuring The Epic Adventurer
Created By **ROBERT E. HOWARD**

**ROY THOMAS** \* **JOHN BUSCEMA** \* **DANNY BULANADI** \* **JOE ROSEN** \* **GEORGE ROUSSOS** \* **LOUISE JONES** \* **JIM SHOOTER**
WRITER/EDITOR / ARTIST/ILLUSTRATOR / INKER/EMBELLISHER / LETTERER / COLORIST / CONSULTING EDITOR / EDITOR-IN-CHIEF

THE BATTLE OF YANYOGA IS OVER\*...THOTH-AMON HAS PERISHED AND SCATTERED LIKE DUST TO THE FOUR WINDS...AND NOW THE ARMY OF AQUILONIA IS HEADED NORTH AGAIN, FROM THE PLACE WHICH MEN CALL THE WORLD'S EDGE...

WHAT'S WRONG, YOUR MAJESTY-- IF I MAY BE SO BOLD?

YOU LOOK FAR TOO SOMBRE FOR A MAN WHO'S RECENTLY SLAIN HIS WORST ENEMY, AND NOW CARRIES NEWS OF THE TRIUMPH BACK TO HIS ROYAL CAPITAL.

\*LAST ISSUE. --ROY.

THAT'S JUST IT, TROCERO...

WE CARRY THAT NEWS FAR TOO SLOWLY TO SUIT ME.

IT'S BEEN WELL NIGH A YEAR, AFTER ALL, THAT I'VE BEEN SEPARATED FROM ZENOBIA.

AH, SO MY KING DOES MISS HIS QUEEN, EH?

I MUST CONFESS, SIRE, I DOUBTED ANY ONE WOMAN COULD EVER MEAN SO MUCH TO YOU.

SO DID I, COUNT. BUT WHEN YOU'VE LIVED WITH A WOMAN SO LONG... HAD THREE CHILDREN BY HER...

WELL, DAMN IT ALL... I MISS HER!

...UNLIKE YOUNG PRINCE CONN BACK THERE, FOR WHOM THIS WAS VERY NEARLY HIS FIRST TASTE OF REAL ADVENTURE!

I'M WHAT YOU CIVILIZED MEN WOULD CALL...HOME-SICK...

THAT NIGHT, **ARMED SENTRIES** PATROL THE OUTER PERIMETERS OF THE AQUILONIAN CAMP...

FOR, **FOOLISH** THE MAN IN THIS HYBORIAN AGE WHO LOWERS HIS **GUARD**, EVEN WHEN ALL HIS FOES SEEM DEAD OR DEFEATED.

WITHIN THE CAMP, HOWEVER, KING CONAN'S MIND IS ELSE-WHERE...

I SWEAR I DON'T **UNDERSTAND** MY FATHER SOMETIMES, COUNT TROCERO...

FROM WHAT LITTLE HE'S TOLD ME, HIS **YOUTH** WAS FULL OF DANGER, EXCITEMENT...AND HE **REVELED** IN IT.

HE'S **STILL** TWICE THE FIGHTER OF ANY MAN ALIVE...

AT **LEAST**, YOUNG PRINCE!

...YET RATHER THAN ADD **NEW CONQUESTS** ON OUR ROAD NORTH, HE MARCHES STRAIGHT FOR HOME LIKE ANY **TWENTY-YEAR-MAN** EAGER ONLY TO COLLECT HIS PENSION!

YOU GREATLY EX-AGGERATE YOUR SIRE'S MOOD, PRINCE CONN...BUT YOU'LL UNDERSTAND MORE, WHEN YOU GET **OLDER**.

OLDER! THAT'S WHAT EVERYONE **ALWAYS** SAYS!

AND ALWAYS **WILL**, BECAUSE IT'S ALWAYS **TRUE**.

YOUR FATHER AND MOTHER, AFTER ALL, HAVE BEEN THROUGH ADVENTURES AS PERILOUS AS EVEN THE **PUR-SUIT OF THOTH-AMON**, YOU KNOW.

YES, I'VE HEARD VAGUE **HINTS** OF THAT, BUT NO ONE HAS EVER TOLD ME THE **FULL** STORY.

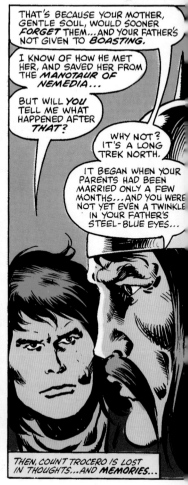

THAT'S BECAUSE YOUR MOTHER, GENTLE SOUL, WOULD SOONER **FORGET** THEM...AND YOUR FATHER'S NOT GIVEN TO **BOASTING**.

I KNOW OF HOW HE MET HER, AND SAVED HER FROM THE **MANOTAUR OF NEMEDIA**...

BUT WILL **YOU** TELL ME WHAT HAPPENED AFTER **THAT**?

WHY NOT? IT'S A LONG TREK NORTH.

IT BEGAN WHEN YOUR PARENTS HAD BEEN MARRIED ONLY A FEW MONTHS...AND YOU WERE NOT YET EVEN A TWINKLE IN YOUR FATHER'S STEEL-BLUE EYES...

THEN, COUNT TROCERO IS LOST IN THOUGHTS...AND **MEMORIES**...

AND WHEN HE SPEAKS AGAIN, HE RELATES HIS TALE ALMOST LIKE ONE IN A TRANCE, FOR WHOM THESE EVENTS ARE OCCURRING **NOW,** NOT NEARLY A DECADE AND A HALF AGONE:

# PROLOGUE:

THE CHAMBER IS MURKY, DARK...AND THE LONG, TAPERS DISPEL THE GLOOM BUT LITTLE.

TO THE WATCHING EYE, IT WOULD BE DIFFICULT TO DISCERN THE **HOODED FIGURE** THAT CROUCHES IN THE MIDDLE OF THE DUSTY, SCROLL-LADEN FLOOR.

NOR IS HE ALONE.

FOR LONG MOMENTS, THEY ENGAGE IN **MUTED SPEECH,** THESE TWO...

...THOUGH FEW MEN OVERHEARING, IF SUCH THERE WERE, WOULD UNDERSTAND SO MUCH AS A SINGLE SYLLABLE OF THE **UNEARTHLY WORDS** WHICH PASS BETWEEN THEM.

THEN, THERE IS A **GUST OF WIND** THROUGH THE ROOM, LIKE THE SWEEP OF **GIGANTIC WINGS.**

THE TAPERS FLICKER MADLY...

...AND THE HOODED FIGURE IS SUDDENLY ALONE, AT LAST.

IT IS A NIGHT FOR *FEASTING* IN *TARANTIA*, CAPITAL OF PROUD *AQUILONIA*.

AND WHY SHOULD IT *NOT* BE? AFTER ALL, IT HAS BEEN MORE THAN A YEAR, SINCE *KING TARASCUS* OF *NEMEDIA*, AIDED BY THE UNDEAD WIZARD *XALTOTUN*, ATTEMPTED TO CONQUER THIS *GREATEST* OF HYBORIAN KINGDOMS.

# THE *RING* OF RAKHAMON!

BEGINNING OUR ADAPTATION OF THE NOVEL *CONAN THE AVENGER*, BY BJÖRN NYBERG & L. SPRAGUE DE CAMP

NO THOUGHT OF PICTS OR NEMEDIANS THIS NIGHT, HOWEVER... FOR THIS IS THE NIGHT KING CONAN GIVES A *ROYAL BALL* IN HONOR OF HIS BELOVED *ZENOBIA*.

NO DOUBT SOME OF THE ASSEMBLED LORDS AND LADIES WHISPER OF HOW THEIR NEW QUEEN WAS ONCE A VIRTUAL *SLAVE* IN THE HAREM OF NEMEDIA'S MURDEROUS RULER.

BUT, SHE HELPED CONAN ESCAPE TARASCUS' DUNGEONS, AND THE GRATEFUL CIMMERIAN-- HIMSELF A USURPER OF THRONES-- HAD MADE HER HIS *WIFE*.

THE NEMEDIAN SCHEME FAILED, HEAVY DAMAGES WERE EXACTED...

AND NOW, THE ONLY DISORDERS ARE THE INTERMITTENT RAIDS OF THE SAVAGE *PICTS* ON THE WESTERN BORDER...RAIDS HELD IN CHECK BY SEASONED TROOPS ALONG THE *THUNDER RIVER.*

HE HAS MASTERED HER *HEART,* THESE PAST FEW MONTHS OF MARRIAGE...

AND SHE, IN TURN, HAS MADE HIM MORE AMENABLE TO THE PLEASANTRIES OF SUCH COURTLY EVENTS AS THIS, WHICH ARE ALIEN TO HIS BARBAROUS NATURE:

'SO *PLEASED* YOU COULD BE HERE THIS EVENING, COUNTESS ALBIONA.

AND YOUR NEW HUSBAND, COUNT NESTOR.

IT IS *MY* PLEASURE, YOUR MAJESTIES, TO DO HOMAGE TO AQUILONIA'S GRACIOUS QUEEN... AND TO MY OWN GOOD *FRIEND.*

AT LENGTH, THE BALL FORMALLY BEGINS...

...LED BY AQUILONIA'S ROYAL COUPLE.

YOU'RE DOING SPLENDIDLY! BUT THEN, I'M PREJUDICED, HAVING TAUGHT YOU THIS PAST WEEK.

PLEASE FORGIVE ME IF I STEP ON YOUR TOES, MY LOVE.

EVERYONE IN THE GLITTERING THRONG FOLLOWS SUIT, TILL COUPLES MILL COLORFULLY ON THE POLISHED FLOOR...

AND NO ONE NOTICES THE *SILENT DRAFT* THAT BEGINS TO WAFT THROUGH THE AIR...

...CAUSING THE FLAMING TORCHES TO FLICKER AND *TREMBLE.*

NOR DOES ANYONE NOTICE THE *BURNING EYES* THAT PEER FROM ABOVE, SWEEPING AN AVID GLANCE OVER THE CROWD...

...FOCUSING UPON THE SLIM, SILVER-SHEATHED FIGURE BESIDE THE KING...

...AS THE MUSIC MOMENTARILY HALTS,

I THINK I'LL STEP OUT ON THE BALCONY FOR A NIP OF FRESH AIR, CONAN.

ALL THIS DANCING HAS WARMED MY BLOOD.

AND *MINE...* THOUGH IN A DIFFERENT WAY. LET US LEAVE.

OH, *YOUR HIGHNESS--* IS IT TRUE WHAT WE'VE BEEN HEARING-- THAT YOU WERE ONCE A SWASHBUCKLING *ZINGARAN BUCCANEER?*

UH... YES, LADIES, AND A BARACHAN *PIRATE,* TOO-- A MORE HONEST NAME FOR IT.

NOW, IF YOU'LL KINDLY EXCUSE ME...

BUT, *I'VE* HEARD YOU WERE ONCE A CHIEFTAIN OF THE WILD HORDES IN HALF-FABULOUS *GHULISTAN,* 'WAY OFF IN THE HIMELIAN MOUNTAINS!

NOT SO! WHAT HE REALLY DID, YEARS AGO, IS SAVE THE *QUEEN OF KHAURAN* FROM A BUNCH OF *SHEMITE PLUNDERERS,* ISN'T THAT RIGHT, SIRE?

I FEAR I MUST PLEAD GUILTY ON *ALL* COUNTS, LADIES.

BECOMING YOUR *KING* IS PROBABLY THE FIRST *HONEST* DAY'S WORK I'VE EVER DONE.

OH, YOUR *MAJESTY*... YOU ARE SO *AMUSING!*

NOW, FORGIVE ME, BUT I REALLY *MUST* JOIN MY QUEEN, SO --

*ZENOBIA!*

OUT OF MY WAY, MAN!

THE SCREAM IS ALREADY *DWINDLING* AS THE BARBARIAN-KING SPRINGS FORWARD, UPSETTING NOBLE GUESTS AND WINE-LADEN TABLES--

--AND, WHEN HE REACHES THE BALCONY IN PANTHER-ISH STRIDES, ONLY SECONDS LATER, ZENOBIA IS--

GONE!?

BUT-- THAT'S *IMPOSSIBLE!*

INSTINCTIVELY, CONAN'S GLANCE RAKES THE UNSCALABLE SIDES OF THE PALACE, BUT SEES... NOTHING.

THEN, AS HE LIFTS HIS GAZE SKYWARD--

*CROM'S DEV'LS!*

ZENOBIA...!

FOR A LONG MOMENT, CONAN STANDS TRANSFIXED.

THEN, AS HE STRIDES BACK INSIDE, HIS GUESTS *SHRINK AWAY* AS IF HE HAS BECOME THE VERY *MONSTER* THAT HAS CARRIED OFF HIS QUEEN.

WORDLESSLY, HE MAKES FOR THE WEAPON-LADEN NETHER *WALL*, WHERE HANGS A PLAIN BUT HEAVY *BROADSWORD* THAT HAS SERVED HIM WELL IN MANY A CAMPAIGN...

AND ONLY THEN DOES HE SPEAK...

FROM THIS HOUR, I AM *NO LONGER* YOUR KING-- UNTIL I HAVE RE-TURNED WITH MY *STOLEN QUEEN!*

IF I CANNOT *SEEK OUT* THIS DEVIL, I AM NOT *FIT* TO RULE!

BUT, BY CROM, I WILL *SEEK OUT* THIS DEVIL, AND WREAK *VENGEANCE* UPON HIM, BE HE PROTECTED BY ALL THE ARMED HOSTS IN THE WORLD!

THEN, OPENING WIDE HIS MOUTH, THE KING VOICES A *WEIRD AND TERRIBLE CALL* THAT ECHOES SHUDDERINGLY THROUGH THE HALL...

IT RINGS LIKE THE CRY OF *DOOMED SOULS*...AND THE EERIE HORROR OF ITS TONES TURNS MANY A FACE ASHEN.

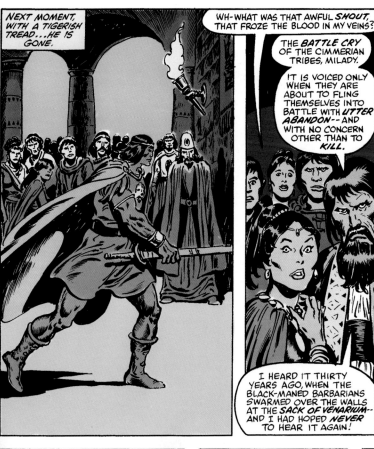

NEXT MOMENT, WITH A TIGERISH TREAD...HE IS GONE.

WH-WHAT WAS THAT AWFUL *SHOUT*, THAT FROZE THE BLOOD IN MY VEINS?

THE *BATTLE CRY* OF THE CIMMERIAN TRIBES, MILADY.

IT IS VOICED ONLY WHEN THEY ARE ABOUT TO FLING THEMSELVES INTO BATTLE WITH *UTTER ABANDON*-- AND WITH NO CONCERN OTHER THAN TO *KILL*.

I HEARD IT THIRTY YEARS AGO, WHEN THE BLACK-MANED BARBARIANS SWARMED OVER THE WALLS AT THE *SACK OF VENARIUM*-- AND I HAD HOPED *NEVER* TO HEAR IT AGAIN!

MINUTES LATER...

BUT MY KING...

NO, PROSPERO-- *NO!* I WILL TRAVEL *ALONE!*

IF I TAKE OUR LEGIONS WITH ME, OUR PEACE-LOVING *NEIGHBOR NATIONS* MAY SEIZE THE CHANCE TO *STRIKE*.

BUT, SIRE-- WE CANNOT LET YOU *RISK YOUR LIFE* ON SUCH AN UNCERTAIN QUEST.

LET *TROCERO* AND ME RIDE WITH YOU, AT LEAST...!

NO, MY GOOD GENERAL AND FRIEND... I FEEL I'M DESTINED TO FREE MY QUEEN *ALONE*.

YOU SHALL COMMAND THE *ARMY* IN MY ABSENCE... TROCERO, THE *KINGDOM*.

IF I'M NOT BACK IN TWO YEARS-- CHOOSE A *NEW KING!*

NOW, A *HORSE*, PROSPERO! I RIDE AT ONCE TO FIND *PELIAS OF KOTH*, WHO DWELLS IN KHANYRIA, IN *KHORAJA*.

WHAT, SIRE? THAT-- *WIZARD!?*

AYE, THAT WIZARD WHO AIDED ME WHEN *TSOTHA-LANTI* HAD DEFEATED AND IMPRISONED ME, SEVERAL YEARS AGO. *

*"THE SCARLET CITADEL" IN SAVAGE SWORD #30. --ROY.

I SMELL *DARK SORCERY* IN TONIGHT'S HAPPENINGS, MY FRIENDS; THAT FLYING CREATURE WAS NO EARTHLY *BIRD*.

I CARE *LITTLE* FOR WIZARDS, CROM AND MITRA KNOW-- BUT NOW I NEED PELIAS' *ADVICE*.

I RIDE TONIGHT-- GARBED AS A COMMON *MERCENARY*.

LOOKING RIGHT AND LEFT TO MAKE CERTAIN HE'S NOT BEEN SEEN, THE MAN DRESSED AS A RETAINER OF THE COURT SLINKS DOWN THE STAIR...

AND SOON, HE IS DARTING AMONG THE NARROW STREETS AND ALLEYWAYS OF THE WESTERN PART OF THE CITY...

...TILL HE COMES TO A LARGE, HIGH-WALLED *HOUSE* WITH BUT A SINGLE DOOR.

HERE, HE KNOCKS FOUR TIMES.

THE DUSKY STYGIAN WHO ANSWERS HIS KNOCK HEARS A FEW WHISPERED WORDS, AND...

THIS WAY...!

WHAT BRINGS YOU *HERE*, MARINUS?

HAVEN'T YOU ENOUGH *SPYING* TO DO FOR ME AT THE *KING'S BALL*--

OR DID THAT USURPING SAVAGE *CALL IT OFF* IN ONE OF HIS BARBARIC MOODS?

GH-GHANDAR CHEN, MY LORD--

THE QUEEN OF AQUILONIA HAS BEEN *ABDUCTED* BY SOME UN-EARTHLY *FLYING MONSTER!*

EVEN NOW, THE KING RIDES *ALONE* TO SEARCH FOR HER--AND HE GOES FIRST TO VISIT THE KOTHIAN SORCERER PELIAS, IN *KHANYRIA*.

BY *ERLIK!* THIS IS *NEWS* INDEED!

FIVE OF MY BEST *POISONERS* HANG ON THE HILL OF *EXECUTION,* SO MUCH KITE'S MEAT--

--BUT NOW, CONAN WILL BE *ALONE*--AND IN *FOREIGN LANDS?!*

YES, MY LORD.

YOU *HEARD,* STYGIAN?

AYE, MY LORD GHANDAR.

RIDE SWIFTLY TO *BARACCUS,* WHO CAMPS ON THE *YIVGA RIVER.*

ORDER HIM TO TAKE AS MANY MEN AS HE NEEDS-- AND *SLAY* CONAN BEFORE HE REACHES THAT SORCERER-- DO YOU *UNDERSTAND?*

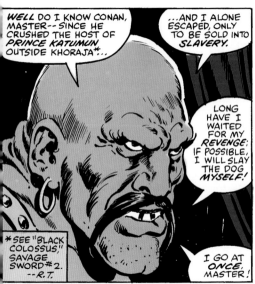

*WELL* DO I KNOW CONAN, MASTER--SINCE HE CRUSHED THE HOST OF *PRINCE KATUMUN* OUTSIDE KHORAJA*...

...AND I ALONE ESCAPED, ONLY TO BE SOLD INTO *SLAVERY.*

LONG HAVE I WAITED FOR MY *REVENGE;* IF POSSIBLE, I WILL SLAY THE DOG *MYSELF!*

*SEE "BLACK COLOSSUS," SAVAGE SWORD #2. --R.T.

I GO AT *ONCE,* MASTER!

THEN, WHEN HIS STYGIAN BONDSERVANT IS GONE, THE MAN CALLED GHUNDAR CHEN TAKES UP GOLDEN PEN AND PARCHMENT...

To King Yezdigerd, lord of Turan and the Eastern Empire...

AND, WHEN HE HAS *FINISHED...*

RIDE SWIFTLY TO *AGHRAPUR,* MARINUS--AND TAKE THIS TO *KING YEZDIGERD* HIMSELF!

HE WILL REWARD US *BOTH* HANDSOMELY, I ASSURE YOU.

YES, MY LORD.

YES...*VERY* HANDSOMELY, INDEED...!

SOME DAYS LATER, WHILE THE SCORCHING AFTERNOON SUN CASTS SEARING RAYS ACROSS THE DESERT...

...A SOLITARY *RIDER*, WEARING A SNOWY KHALAT, HALTS WITHIN SIGHT OF DOMED BUILDINGS AND TOWERING WALLS.

*KHANYRIA!*

I'D THANK *CROM*— BUT I DOUBT MY SAVAGE NORTHERN GOD HELPED ME IN THE FIRST PLACE.

I JUST HOPE PELIAS IS IN HIS *FULL SENSES*, NOT LYING DRUNK ON HIS GOLDEN DIVAN.

WELL, IF HE IS, BY BADB, I'LL *WAKEN* HIM!

IN THE COBBLED MARKETPLACE OF THIS KHORAJAN CITY, A *MOTLEY THRONG* SWIRLS AND EDDIES...

AND, AT ITS WESTERN GATE...

I TELL YOU, LAD, WE'RE GETTING *STRANGER* WAYFARERS IN THIS CITY EVERY DAY!

UH... DON'T LOOK *NOW*, CAPTAIN CRASSIDES...

...BUT I DOUBT EVEN *YOU*'VE SEEN ANY STRANGER THAN *THIS* GROUP!

IT IS NOT THE CUSTOM OF THE KHANYRIAN CITY GUARD TO HALT POSSIBLE WOULD-BE *TRADERS* WITHOUT GOOD REASON.

HMMMMPH...!

STILL, CRASSIDES IS GLAD WHEN THE SEVEN MEN, MOSTLY TURANIANS, DISAPPEAR INTO THE PROFUSION OF *SMOKY TAVERNS* BEYOND.

168

THEN, EVEN AS THE SUN GLOWS ITS LAST...

LET ME *IN*, GATESMAN!

WHAT *SEEK* YOU HERE, ROGUE?

WE LET *NO OUTLANDERS* IN AT NIGHT, TO CUT OUR THROATS!

MY FRIEND...FOR WORDS LESS THAN THOSE, I HAVE SLIT A HUNDRED GULLETS.

*LET ME IN*-- OR BY CROM, I'LL RAISE A *HORDE* TO SACK THIS BUNCH OF HOVELS!

NO NEED FOR *ANGER*, HORSEMAN; THIS GUARD IS *NEW*.

*WHAT* IS YOUR *BUSINESS* IN OUR CITY?

CALL ME *ARUS*-- AND I SEEK *PELIAS*, THE SORCERER.

YOU MAY ENTER!

MOMENTS LATER, THE NEWCOMER CANTERS THROUGH...

...NOT DEIGNING EVEN TO GLANCE AT THOSE AROUND THE GATE.

WHY DID YOU LET HIM *IN*, CAPTAIN CRASSIDES? HE'S A *NORTHERN BARBARIAN*, FROM HIS LOOK AND ACCENT!

LIKE *ANOTHER* I HEARD OF, SOME YEARS AGO...

...WHO ONCE LED A BAND OF OUTLAW *ZUAGIRS** AGAINST THE SHEMITE CITY-STATES SOUTH OF HERE.

*FIERCE DESERT NOMADS.--R.T.

*THIS* FELLOW MIGHT BE ONE OF THAT SORT,... THOUGH HARDLY THE *SAME MAN*, OF COURSE.

BUT *ALONE*, HE CAN DO US LITTLE HARM, WHATEVER HIS INTENT.

AND IF HE MEANS US *ILL*-- WHY, THEN, *PELIAS* WILL KNOW IT BY HIS ARCANE ARTS AND TAKE PROPER MEASURES.

*NOW* DO YOU BEGIN TO SEE?

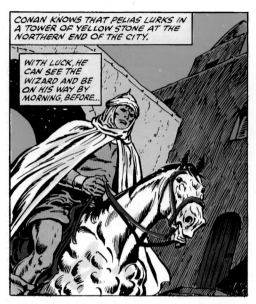

CONAN KNOWS THAT PELIAS LURKS IN A TOWER OF YELLOW STONE AT THE NORTHERN END OF THE CITY.

WITH LUCK, HE CAN SEE THE WIZARD AND BE ON HIS WAY BY MORNING, BEFORE...

HELP!

IN THE NAME OF ISHTAR -- HELP ME!

W-WILL YOU HELP ME, KIND SIR? I-- I--

WHAT'S WRONG, LASS?

IS YOUR LOVER ANGRY WITH YOU, OR WHAT?

PLEASE, SIR-- DON'T JEST WITH ME--

WHAT IS IT, THEN? SPEAK UP.

T-TWO DRUNKEN SOLDIERS-- IN YONDER TAVERN!

THEY TOOK MY MONEY-- TRIED TO-- TO--

STEADY, LASS! WE'LL PULL THEIR BEARDS YET.

ARE THOSE TWO LOUTS THE ONLY GUESTS WITHIN THE TAVERN?

YES, BUT--

THEN STAND ASIDE, AND OUT OF HARM'S WAY, GIRL!

I'VE OTHER BUSINESS HERE IN KHANYRIA, BUT I'M CURSED IF I'LL STAND BY AND LET--

EH? WHY DO YOU *SHUT THE DOOR* BEHIND ME, LASS? ARE YOU AFRAID THAT--

MITRA *CURSE* ME FOR A MUTTON-BRAINED *FOOL!*

A *TRAP!*

A *CIVILIZED* MAN WOULD BE STUNNED BY SURPRISE ONE SECOND AT SUCH A SIGHT--

--THEN *CUT DOWN* THE NEXT, AS ARMED MEN RUSHED SWIFTLY UPON HIM--

*SLAY HIM!*

--BUT NOT THE GIANT CIMMERIAN. *HERE,* TURANIAN DOGS!

UNNNH--!

OWWWW!

ALREADY, CONAN IS *COUNTING.*

EVEN IN THE TWILIGHT GLOOM, CONAN'S SHARP EYES CAN SEE THERE ARE *SEVEN* ALIGNED AGAINST HIM.

TWO ARE DONE FOR THE MOMENT, NURSING PAINFUL BRUISES...

...AND THIS **THIRD** WILL STAY DOWN EVEN LONGER.

ARRRR

STILL, THERE IS NO TIME FOR CONAN TO DRAW HIS GREAT SWORD...

YET, WITH A MUSCLE-WRENCHING **HEAVE**--

--HE INSTANTLY MAKES USE OF WHAT'S AT HAND.

AND **NOW** HE HAS TIME TO UNSHEATHE HIS BLADE!

A **RED MIST** SWIMS BEFORE HIS EYES--HIS BARBARIAN BLOOD ROUSED BY THIS TREACHEROUS AMBUSH--

--AND, WHEN ONE OF THE FLAILING TURANIANS REACHES FOR HIS OWN FALLEN WEAPON--

--CONAN GIVES HIM *CRUSHED RIBS* TO NURSE FOR THE NEXT *SIXMONTH.*

YOWWWRR

THAT LEAVES BUT *THREE* IN FIGHTING CONDITION, HE MUSES...

...NO, *TWO!*

AAAAAa

THEN, AT LAST, WORDS FROM OTHER LIPS THAN CONAN'S OWN...

I *SWORE* THIS DAY WOULD COME, YOU LOW-BORN DOG!

I *KNOW* THAT VOICE, BY THE GODS!

*BARACCUS!* BUT YOU'RE AN *AQUILONIAN* BORN, THOUGH YOU NOW WEAR THE LIVERY OF A *TURANIAN!*

AYE! YOU *EXILED* ME, LONG MONTHS AGO, FOR PLOTTING WITH THE *OPHIREANS* AGAINST YOU.

NOW, I'LL *EVEN* THAT SCORE!

YOU SHOULD HAVE ATTACKED ME IN *BROAD DAYLIGHT,* TRAITOROUS FOOL...

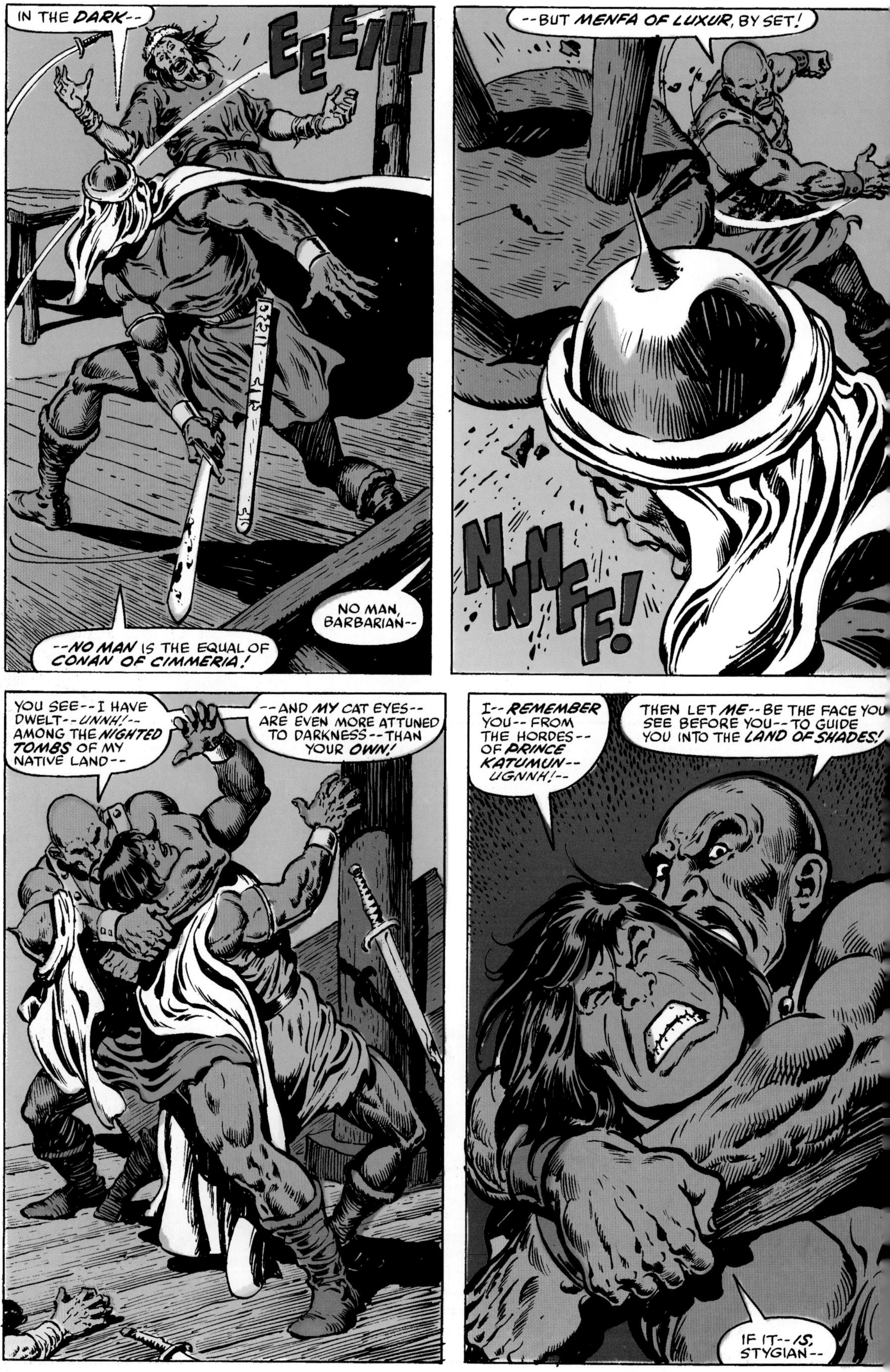
IN THE DARK--
EEEIIII
--NO MAN IS THE EQUAL OF CONAN OF CIMMERIA!
NO MAN, BARBARIAN--
--BUT MENFA OF LUXUR, BY SET!
NNNFF!
YOU SEE--I HAVE DWELT--UNNH!--AMONG THE NIGHTED TOMBS OF MY NATIVE LAND--
--AND MY CAT EYES--ARE EVEN MORE ATTUNED TO DARKNESS--THAN YOUR OWN!
I--REMEMBER YOU--FROM THE HORDES--OF PRINCE KATUMUN--UGNNH!--
THEN LET ME--BE THE FACE YOU SEE BEFORE YOU--TO GUIDE YOU INTO THE LAND OF SHADES!
IF IT--IS, STYGIAN--

--IT WILL BE BECAUSE *YOU* ARE THERE FOR MANY YEARS--

--*BEFORE* ME!

OOOFF!

NOW, YOU SCHEMING DEVIL--

--THE TABLES ARE *TURNED!*

TELL ME WHO-- *MMMFF!*--SENT YOU AFTER ME, OR I'LL--

BUT THE GREAT-MUSCLED STYGIAN *FIGHTS BACK* DESPERATELY--AND CONAN KNOWS IT IS *KILL OR BE KILLED.*

AND WHEN THAT IS THE CHOICE...FOR THE CIMMERIAN, IT IS *NO* CHOICE AT ALL.

*MURDEROUS JACKAL!*

BUT MENFA OF LUXUR CAN NO LONGER HEAR.

INDEED, SEVERAL ARE DEAD, THE OTHERS FLED, WHEN ABRUPTLY--

OH, MERCY...

--WHAT HAS HAPPENED TO MY *FINE HOUSE?*

BLOOD ALL OVER-- FURNITURE *RUINED*--!

*YOU* HAD A HAND IN THIS, YOU YAPPING DOG!

THEY COULDN'T HAVE SET THIS AMBUSH WITHOUT YOUR *HELP!*

M-MERCY, MILORD! THEY TH-THREATENED TO CUT MY *THROAT* OTHERWISE-- I *SWEAR* THEY DID--!

ENOUGH! BE GLAD I DON'T FLAY YOU ALIVE!

NOW, FETCH SOME FOOD AND DRINK-- ALSO SOME CLEAN CLOTHS TO BIND UP THESE SCRATCHES!

YES-- YES, MILORD!

...KILLING DRIES A MAN'S THROATS, BY CROM.

NOW, TELL ME,-- WHERE'S THE GIRL WHO WAS HERE WITH THESE MEN BEFORE I ENTERED?

MILORD, AGAIN I SWEAR TO YOU--

-- I NEVER SAW HER UNTIL SHE CAME HERE YESTERDAY, DRESSED IN OUT-LANDISH GARMENTS. SHE--

LEAD ME TO HER ROOM-- AT ONCE! AND, SHOULD THIS PROVE ANOTHER TRAP--!

IT WON'T, MILORD-- I SWEAR IT.

YOU SWEAR TOO MUCH, TAVERNER. JUST SHOW ME HER ROOM!

YES...

HERE IT IS, GOOD SIR.

OPEN THE DOOR WIDE-- SO I CAN SEE CLEARLY BEFORE I ENTER!

GOOD! THE ROOM'S TOO SMALL FOR A SECOND AMBUSH.

THE GIRL CHANGED HER GARB IN THIS ROOM, MILORD, AS YOU CAN PLAINLY SEE.

AS ISHTAR IS MY WITNESS, I KNOW NOTHING ELSE ABOUT HER!

EASY, MAN. I BELIEVE YOU. NOW GO!

BUT, AS CONAN LOOKS AT THE GLEAMING SILKS...A TURBAN STRIP WITH AN EMERALD PIN...A FILMY VEIL....HE STANDS SILENT WITH STARTLED RECOGNITION.

THIS IS THE GARB OF A TURANIAN NOBLEWOMAN... FROM THE GREAT EASTERN EMPIRE OF KING YEZDIGERD!

AS HE RIDES FORTH, SOON AFTERWARD, ONLY A LITTLE STIFFENED BY WOUNDS WHICH WOULD FELL AN ORDINARY MAN FOR DAYS, CONAN IS PUZZLED.

HE KNOWS WELL THAT **MANY** MEN OF DIFFERENT CREEDS, RACES, AND STATION LUST FOR HIS BLOOD.

ONLY **TROCERO** AND **PROSPERO** KNEW OF HIS MISSION AND DESTINATION, HOWEVER...AND THEIR LOYALTY IS BEYOND QUESTION.

STILL, SOMETHING OR SOMEONE BROUGHT BARACCUS FROM THE **WEST** AND THE TURANIAN WOMAN FROM THE **EAST** TOGETHER TO TRY TO SLAY HIM.

BUT NOW, EMERGING UPON A WIDE, DESERTED SQUARE, HE SPIES THE OUTLINE OF A **SPIRED EDIFICE**, POINTING LIKE A GOLDEN ARROW AIMED AT HEAVEN'S HEART...

THE TOWER WHERE **PELIAS** SECRETS HIMSELF FROM THE UNDESIRED COMPANY OF HIS FELLOW MAN!

A BROAD EXPANSE OF TRIMMED GARDENS AND LAWNS SURROUNDS THE GREAT YELLOW TOWER...BUT **NO GATES** ARE PRESENT, OR NEEDED.

AFTER ALL, **HORRID LEGENDS**, BIRTHED IN TRUTH, HAVE TAUGHT THE MEN OF KHANYRIA TO KEEP AWAY FROM THIS WIZARD'S ABODE.

AYE, MEN...

177

...BUT WHAT COULD THUS AFFECT CONAN'S *MOUNT?*

YOU DON'T LIKE SORCERERS MUCH *EITHER,* DO YOU?

*WHOA,* BOY!

CAN'T SAY I *BLAME* YOU MUCH.

PERHAPS, HE MUSES AS HE STALKS TOWARD THE TOWER, PELIAS HAS UN-HOLY *COMPANY* THIS NIGHT...

FOR, NECROMANTIC RITES OFTEN DRAW *NAMELESS* MON-STROSITIES TO THEM, AS THE SMELL OF CARRION ATTRACTS VULTURES.

THE CIMMERIAN HAS MET HIS SHARE OF SUCH.

REACHING THE TOWER, HE NOTES THAT ITS COLOR IS CAUSED BY AN ABUNDANCE OF *SMALL GOLDEN COINS* SET IN PLASTER.

NONE OF THE COINS LOOK FAMILIAR... AND ALL HAVE THE LOOK OF *GREAT AGE.*

CONAN KNOWS THAT SUCH ANCIENT GOLD IS CONSIDERED QUITE VALUABLE IN *MAKING MAGIC...* AND HE SHIVERS.

ALL THE SAME, HE TRIES THE *IRON DOOR...*

...WHICH SWINGS SILENTLY INWARD.

BY THE FAINT LIGHT COMING THROUGH THE OPEN DOOR, CONAN CAN SEE ONE FLIGHT OF STAIRS CIRCLING *UPWARD,* TOWARD THE TOP OF THE TOWER.

ANOTHER, NEAR AT HAND, LOSES ITSELF IN UNDERGROUND *DARK-NESS....* AND MUSKY *ODORS* WAFT UP FROM A MAZE OF CAVERNS BENEATH THE TOWER.

THE CIMMERIAN IS RECALLING SIMILAR ODORS IN THE HAUNTED CATACOMBS OF THE DEAD CITY OF *PTEION,* IN STYGIA, WHEN SUDDENLY--

*WELCOME,* CONAN! MOUNT THE STAIRS LEADING UPWARD-- AND FOLLOW THE *LIGHT.*

PELIAS? WHERE ARE YOU, MAN-- IF IT'S YOU?

AND *WHAT* LIGHT ARE YOU--?

MACHA AND NEMAIN!

WITHOUT WARNING, A *SWIRL OF LIGHT* APPEARS BEFORE HIS VERY EYES...

...SWIFTLY FORMING ITSELF INTO A *GLOWING BALL.*

PELIAS-- I *LIKE NOT* THIS KIND OF MUMMERY, AS YOU KNOW WELL!

PELIAS...?

AS THE FLOATING, SHIMMERING GLOBE OF LIGHT MOVES SLOWLY UP THE UN-CREAKING STAIRS, CONAN FOLLOWS IT WITHOUT HESITATION.

AND IF SOME *PHANTOM FEAR* GNAWS INWARDLY AT HIS HEART... WHY, HE STILL HIDES IT FAR BETTER THAN MOST.

THEN, AT STAIRS' END, A *RUNE-CARVED DOOR* OPENS SILENTLY...

AND, AS CONAN STEPS THROUGH IT, SENSES FINE-WHETTED LIKE THOSE OF A PROWLING LEOPARD...

...THE LIGHT SIMPLY... *VANISHES.*

OR, RATHER... SOMEONE HAS TAKEN ITS PLACE.

AH, *WELCOME,* CONAN!

HOW LONG HAS IT BEEN? *FOUR* YEARS? *FIVE?*

*FOUR AND A HALF,* PELIAS.

180

BUT, I SEE YOU ARE *WOUNDED*...AND LATELY, TOO.

DRINK *THIS*, MY FRIEND. IT IS MADE FROM THE SECRET HERBS OF THE MISTY ISLES AND OF THE LANDS BEYOND KUSH.

IT WILL *HEAL* YOUR WOUNDS, AND EASE YOUR TIRED MUSCLES.

*HUHN!* MY *VEINS*-- THEY SEEM AFIRE--!

ONLY FOR A *MOMENT*, YOU *SEE*?

YES! ALREADY A VAST *WEARINESS* SEEMS LIFTED FROM MY SHOULDERS.

TRULY, PELIAS, THIS IS A *MAGICAL* BREW!

YES, IT IS RATHER POTENT...A COMPENDIUM OF RARE INGREDIENTS AND POWERFUL INCANTATIONS.

I WISH I'D POSSESSED IT MANY A *FORMER* TIME IN MY LIFE!

STILL, YOU DID *NOT* RIDE SO MANY LEAGUES FROM THE ROYAL PALACE OF AQUILONIA SIMPLY TO PARTAKE OF MY HOSPITALITY.

WHAT *BRINGS* YOU HERE, BOTH ALONE AND IN HASTE?

I'VE NOT HEARD OF ANY GREAT *WARS* IN THE NORTHWEST, IN WHICH YOU MIGHT NEED MY AID.

IF IT WERE ONLY A STRAIGHTFORWARD *WAR*, I WOULD NEVER ASK MAGICAL HELP.

BUT I FIND MYSELF PITTED AGAINST *DARK AND UNKNOWN POWERS*, PELIAS...

I NEED CLUES TO LEAD ME TO WHERE I CAN *SMITE* MY FOE--

--AYE, AND RESCUE MY *QUEEN*-- THE WOMAN I *LOVE*!

IN SHORT SWIFT SENTENCES, CONAN TELLS THE WIZARD OF THE RECENT FATEFUL NIGHT IN TARANTIA...

181

FOR A LONG WHILE, PELIAS BROODS, CHIN IN HAND. THEN...

A *DEMON* OF THE DARKEST REALMS BEYOND THE *MOUNTAINS OF THE NIGHT* HAS STOLEN YOUR MATE, KING CONAN.

*I* KNOW HOW TO SUMMON ONE...

...BUT I THOUGHT I SHARED THAT KNOWLEDGE WITH NO ONE *ELSE* IN THE WEST.

THEN *FETCH* THIS FIEND YOU'RE TALKING ABOUT-- AND WE'LL WRING THE *TRUTH* OUT OF HIM, DEVIL OR NO!

NOT SO FAST, MY HOT-HEADED FRIEND!

DO NOT RUSH HEAD-LONG INTO UNKNOWN *DANGERS.*

IT IS CLEAR THIS DEMON HAS BEEN SUMMONED BY A SORCERER WITH POWERS *SUPERIOR* TO THOSE OF ORDINARY MAGICIANS.

SHOULD WE DRAG THE FIEND HITHER, WE SHOULD HAVE BOTH HIM *AND* HIS MASTER TO COPE WITH...

AND THAT MIGHT BE *TOO MUCH* EVEN FOR US.

NO... I KNOW A *BETTER* WAY.

THE *MIRROR OF LAZBEKRI* SHALL GIVE US THE ANSWER!

DESPITE THE WIZARD'S CRYPTIC GESTURES AND THE BILLOWING BLUE SMOKE, IT SEEMS AS IF NOTHING HAPPENS FOR AN AGE...AN ETERNITY...

THE SORCERER'S DEFENSES ARE *STRONG,* CONAN; I CANNOT PIERCE THEM.

THAT WOULD BE *CROM,* THE GRIM GOD OF THE CIMMERIANS... THOUGH I'VE HAD NOTHING TO DO WITH GODS FOR MANY YEARS.

WHO IS YOUR TUTELARY *DEITY?*

I LEAVE THEM ALONE... AND THEY LEAVE *ME* ALONE.

WELL, *PRAY* TO YOUR CROM FOR HELP. WE *NEED* IT.

CONAN CLOSES HIS EYES AND, FOR THE FIRST TIME IN DECADES...HE PRAYS.

O FATHER CROM, WHO BREATHES POWER TO STRIVE AND SLAY INTO A MAN'S SOUL AT BIRTH...HELP YOUR SON AGAINST THE *DEMON* THAT HAS STOLEN HIS MATE...!

AND IN HIS BRAIN, HE SEEMS TO HEAR...A *VOICE*...

...A VOICE WHICH SAYS: 'LONG HAVE YOU FORSAKEN ME, O CONAN... BUT YOU ARE MY TRUE SON FOR ALL THAT, IN YOUR STRIVING AND ENDURING AND CONQUERING. *BEHOLD!*'

AND, OPENING HIS EYES, CONAN NOTICES FOR THE FIRST TIME THAT THE NEARBY MIRROR SHOWS *NO REFLECTION,* EITHER OF PELIAS OR OF ANYTHING ELSE.

IN A LOW MONOTONE, THE OLD WIZARD CHANTS AN INCANTATION...

OMBOS SUTEKH NUBT... URT-HIKEU KAMEPHIS... KHEPRI HARMAKHIS... *OMBOS SUTEKH NUBT...*

...AND THE CIMMERIAN RECOGNIZES THE TONGUE AS THE LANGUAGE USED BY THE *PRIESTS OF STYGIA* IN THEIR CLANDESTINE RITUALS IN DARK-WALLED *KHEMI!*

THEN, SLOWLY, AN *IMAGE* FORMS IN THE GREY MIRROR.

AT FIRST, IT IS BLURRED... UNCERTAIN...

THEN, WITH ABRUPT SWIFTNESS, IT CLEARS, SHARPENS-- INTO A *COWLED* AND *ROBED* FIGURE, SEATED AT A LOW TABLE, A *SCROLL* IN HIS HANDS.

NEXT INSTANT, THE FIGURE THROWS UP ITS HEAD TO LOOK FULL IN THEIR FACES--

--AND THIN, COLORLESS LIPS PART IN A GHASTLY *GRIN!*

PELIAS-- WHAT THE DEVIL--?

BUT THE KOTHIAN WIZARD DOES NOT RESPOND...

...AS, FROM THE FOLDS OF HIS ROBE, THE GOLD-SKINNED ONE BRINGS FORTH A *SHINING, GLIMMERING BALL.*

HIS OBLIQUE EYES GAZING COLDLY INTO THEIRS, HE RAISES HIS HAND TO *THROW IT--*

CONAN EXPLODES INTO LIGHTNING ACTION--

AND, A MOMENT LATER, THE REFLECTING SURFACE OF THE MIRROR IS SHATTERED INTO THOUSANDS OF TINKLING SPLINTERS!

BY ISHTAR, CONAN-- YOU *SAVED* US BOTH!

THAT SHINING GLOBE WAS AS DEADLY AS A NEST OF COBRAS.

HAD HE MANAGED TO HURL IT INTO *THIS* CHAMBER, WHILE I WAS TOO *SPELLBOUND* TO PREVENT HIM--!

THE DEVIL WITH THAT! WHO WAS THAT MAN, WHO LOOKED TO BE FROM *KHITAI*?

MY FRIEND, THESE MATTERS ARE *DEEPER* THAN I THOUGHT.

THE FATE OF ALL THE *WORLD* MAY REST UPON YOUR *BROAD* SHOULDERS.

AND WHAT HAS HE TO DO WITH MY *QUEST*?

I KNOW NOTHING ABOUT ANY OF THAT, PELIAS.

I JUST WANT *ZENOBIA* BACK!

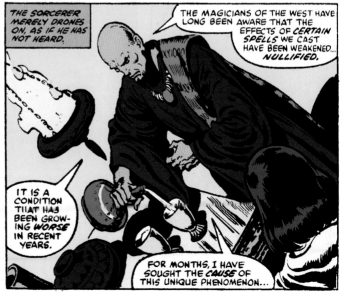

THE SORCERER MERELY DRONES ON, AS IF HE HAS NOT HEARD.

THE MAGICIANS OF THE WEST HAVE LONG BEEN AWARE THAT THE EFFECTS OF *CERTAIN* SPELLS WE CAST HAVE BEEN WEAKENED... *NULLIFIED.*

IT IS A CONDITION THAT HAS BEEN GROW-ING *WORSE* IN RECENT YEARS.

FOR MONTHS, I HAVE SOUGHT THE *CAUSE* OF THIS UNIQUE PHENOMENON...

185

...AND AT LAST, I FEAR I HAVE *FOUND* IT, MAY THE GODS HAVE MERCY ON MY SOUL!

WHAT *ARE* YOU TALKING ABOUT, WIZARD-- AND WHAT HAS THIS TO DO WITH ME AND MY KIDNAPED *WIFE*?

YOU ARE *KING IN AQUILONIA*, MY FRIEND -- THAT PROUD NATION WHICH STANDS AS A *BULWARK* AMONG THE WESTERN NATIONS.

I'M KING, YES...BUT IF I'M SLAIN ON MY QUEST, AQUILONIA WILL HAVE A *NEW* KING...

...AND MY NAME WILL BE FORGOTTEN.

THE ONE IN THE MIRROR HAS FATHOMED THAT *YOU* ARE THE KEY TO HIS CONQUEST OF THE HYBORIAN LANDS.

AYE? YOU ARE *MAD*, PELIAS!

NAY, CIMMERIAN! YOU HAVE LONG BEEN THE *CENTER* OF MIGHTY HAPPENINGS-- AND THE GODS LOOK FAVORABLY UPON YOU.

BY REJUVENATING AQUILONIA, YOU HAVE *FRAYED* THE FAR-FLUNG WEB OF INTRIGUE AND EVIL SPUN BY THE SORCEROUS FORCES OF THE *DISTANT EAST*.

THAT'S WHY HE CONJURED UP A *DEMON* TO CAPTURE YOUR QUEEN.

HE? YOU MEAN--?

THE ONE IN THE *MIRROR*, YES! HE IS CERTAIN YOU WILL BE *SLAIN* BY FOES ALONG THE WAY, AS YOU RIDE TO RESCUE HER.

I CANNOT TALK YOU INTO GOING BACK *HOME* TO TARANTIA, I SUPPOSE...AND LETTING *OTHERS* SEEK YOUR MATE FOR YOU?

GO TO THE *DEVIL*, PELIAS!

THAT'S WHAT I THOUGHT YOU'D SAY... AND SO, *HERE*!

MANY MOONS HAVE PASSED SINCE I WON THIS *RING*, FROM A POWERFUL SORCERER OF LUXUR.

THROUGH EONS OF BLACK TIME I STROVE WITH HIM-- BUT THOSE WERE THE DAYS WHEN I WAS *YOUNG*, AND GLORIED IN MY POWERS.

NOW, MY FRIEND, I WANT *YOU* TO WEAR THIS RING ON YOUR JOURNEY--

THE *RING OF RAKHAMON!*

YOU HAVE *HEARD* OF RAKHAMON, OF COURSE?

WHO HAS *NOT* HEARD OF THAT DREAD SORCERER, THOUGH HE PERISHED A CENTURY AND A HALF AGO?

HE FASHIONED THIS RING, IT'S SAID, OF A *FALLEN STAR* HE FOUND IN THE FROZEN NORTH.

AYE, THAT'S IT. PUT IT ON.

I FEEL-- SO--

*STRANGE?* AND WELL YOU SHOULD! IT'S SAID RAKHAMON NEEDED THE RING TO *CONTROL* SOME OF THE MORE UN- YIELDING DEMONS HE SUMMONED FORTH...

WE SOON SHALL SEE!

PELIAS! WHAT THE DEVIL--?

BEFORE THE RING CAN SERVE YOU, CONAN, YOU FIRST MUST PROVE *WORTHY* OF IT.

ALREADY THE RING *DRAWS* YOU TO A PLACE WHICH IS NOT A PLACE...SO THAT YOUR *TESTING* MAY BEGIN...!

PELIAS! CURSE YOU, WIZARD--

HOW MAY I *USE* THE RING? *HOW??*

THERE IS NO ANSWER, AS CONAN FINDS HIMSELF STANDING WHERE THERE IS NEITHER EARTH BELOW, NOR SKY ABOVE...

...BUT ONLY IMMATERIAL, HOWLING *SPIRITS*...

...AND THEN, STRIDING FROM THE DARKNESS, THERE IS SUDDENLY--

--SOME- THING ELSE!

CROM PRESERVE ME!

EVEN AS THE CLAWED THING GRASPS HIS THROAT--

--HE SUDDENLY REALIZES HE IS GARBED NO LONGER AS AQUILONIA'S KING--

--BUT AS THE *WANDERER* THAT ONCE HE WAS--

--THE WARRIOR CALLED CONAN THE CIMMERIAN!

AND WITH THAT REALIZATION COMES A STIRRING TO LIFE--

--AN END TO THE HORROR-STRUCK PARALYSIS WHICH HAD GRIPPED HIM IN THIS NETHER DOMAIN.

THE THING HE FACES IS MUTE--AND CONAN WONDERS, ALMOST, IF THERE CAN BE SOUND IN SUCH A PLACE...

THEN, AS HE HEARS BONES GRIND AND CRACK BENEATH INHUMAN FLESH, HE KNOWS THAT IT CAN!

AND HE KNOWS... MORE.

HAH! IF YOUR BONES CAN BREAK, MONSTER--

--YOU CAN BE SLAIN, IF I'M STRONG ENOUGH--AND FAST ENOUGH!

THE BARBARIAN KNOWS HIS ONLY CHANCE IS TO GET BEHIND THE HELLISH CREATURE--

--TO KEEP OUT OF REACH OF THOSE FLAILING ARMS, THOSE CLACKING PINCERS!

BUT, THE THING'S NECK AND SPINE ARE THICKER AND STRONGER BY FAR THAN EVEN THE NECK OF THE SACRIFICIAL BULL WHICH CONAN SLEW ON HIS DAY OF MANHOOD, SO MANY YEARS AGO...

NOR IS THE DEMON CONTENT TO RELY UPON SHEER STRENGTH ALONE.

MITRA!

THE FLAMES BELOW ARE BLUE-WHITE WITH HEAT--BEYOND ANY THAT HE HAS EVER KNOWN--

YET, THOUGH HE FEELS HIS SKIN BLISTERING, *BURNING*-- SMELLS HIS OWN FLESH COOKING, SPLITTING IN THE MADDEN- ING HEAT--

--CONAN *FIGHTS ON.*

IF I MUST *DIE*-- IN THIS HELLISH PLACE--

--THEN LET IT BE IN *BATTLE!*

AND, FLINGING BACK HIS HEAD, HE GIVES ONCE MORE THE *CIMMERIAN WAR-CRY* HE VOICED DAYS AGO IN THE ROYAL PALACE IN TARANTIA--

--A SHOUT THAT SEEMS TO ECHO DOWN THE DARK CORRIDORS OF TIME ITSELF--

--THEN CASCADES *BACK* UPON HIM, AS IF IT HAS HURLED ITSELF AGAINST THE FARTHEST BOUNDARIES OF THE *UNIVERSE*--

--AND NOT BEEN FOUND WANTING.

I AM *ALIVE,* THEN-- AND *WHOLE?*

IT SEEMS YOU HAVE *PASSED* THE RING'S OWN TEST, MY FRIEND.

THAT IS GOOD, FOR THE *FOE* YOU SEEK IS A GREATER SORCERER THAN ANY OF US IN THE *WEST.*

ONLY WITH THE RING'S AID CAN YOU HOPE TO PREVAIL, OR EVEN *SURVIVE*...

...WHEN YOU FACE *YAH CHIENG,* WHO DWELLS IN PAIKING IN FAR-OFF *KHITAI.*

YAH CHIENG? THAT, THEN IS THE NAME OF THE SORCERER WHO HAS TAKEN *ZENOBIA?*

AYE.

THEN, BEFORE I DEPART FOR THE EAST TOMORROW, I'LL SACRIFICE A BULLOCK TO *CROM.*

SAY NOTHING OF IT, LEST PEOPLE THINK CONAN GROWS RELIGIOUS IN HIS OLD AGE.

WITH THE DAWN, I RIDE FOR *KHITAI.*

I'LL NOT REST TILL MY WOMAN -- MY *QUEEN*-- IS RESTORED TO ME--

--AND YAH CHIENG LIES *DEAD* AT MY FEET!

NEXT: *THE ROAD TO KHITAI!*

189

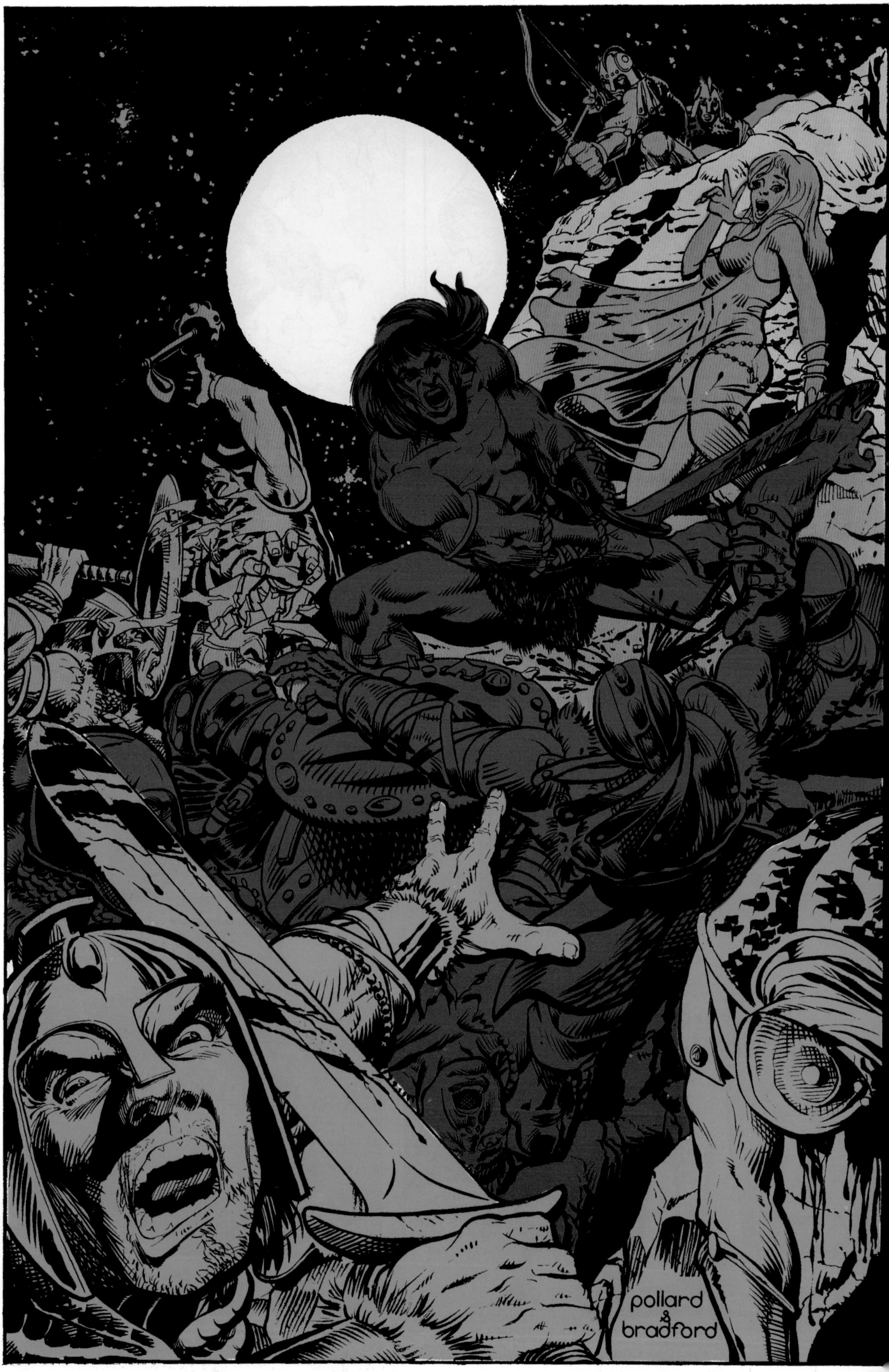
pollard & bradford

# THE CHRONICLES OF CONAN
*Roy Thomas, Barry Windsor-Smith, Gil Kane, John Buscema, Neal Adams, Howard Chaykin, and others*

**Volume 1: Tower of the Elephant and Other Stories**
ISBN 978-1-59307-016-8 | $15.99

**Volume 2: Rogues in the House and Other Stories**
ISBN 978-1-59307-023-6 | $15.99

**Volume 3: The Monster of the Monoliths and Other Stories**
ISBN 978-1-59307-024-3 | $15.99

**Volume 4: The Song of Red Sonja and Other Stories**
ISBN 978-1-59307-025-0 | $15.99

**Volume 5: The Shadow in the Tomb and Other Stories**
ISBN 978-1-59307-175-2 | $15.99

**Volume 6: The Curse of the Golden Skull and Other Stories**
ISBN 978-1-59307-274-2 | $15.99

**Volume 7: The Dweller in the Pool and Other Stories**
ISBN 978-1-59307-300-8 | $15.99

**Volume 8: Brothers of the Blade and Other Stories**
ISBN 978-1-59307-349-7 | $16.99

**Volume 9: Riders of the River-Dragons and Other Stories**
ISBN 978-1-59307-394-7 | $16.99

**Volume 10: When Giants Walk the Earth and Other Stories**
ISBN 978-1-59307-490-6 | $16.99

**Volume 11: The Dance of the Skull and Other Stories**
ISBN 978-1-59307-636-8 | $16.99

**Volume 12: The Beast King of Abombi and Other Stories**
ISBN 978-1-59307-778-5 | $16.99

**Volume 13: Whispering Shadows and Other Stories**
ISBN 978-1-59307-837-9 | $16.99

**Volume 14: Shadow of the Beast and Other Stories**
ISBN 978-1-59307-899-7 | $16.99

**Volume 15: The Corridor of Mullah-Kajar and Other Stories**
ISBN 978-1-59307-971-0 | $16.99

**Volume 16: The Eternity War and Other Stories**
ISBN 978-1-59582-176-8 | $16.99

**Volume 17: The Creation Quest and Other Stories**
ISBN 978-1-59582-177-5 | $17.99

**Volume 18: Isle of the Dead**
ISBN 978-1-59582-382-3 | $17.99

**Volume 19: Deathmark and Other Stories**
ISBN 978-1-59582-515-5 | $17.99

**Volume 20: Night of the Wolf and Other Stories**
ISBN 978-1-59582-584-1 | $18.99

# CONAN MINISERIES
**Conan and the Jewels of Gwahlur**
HARDCOVER
*P. Craig Russell*
ISBN 978-1-59307-491-3 | $13.99

**Conan and the Demons of Khitai**
*Akira Yoshida and Paul Lee*
ISBN 978-1-59307-543-9 | $12.99

**Conan: Book of Thoth**
*Kurt Busiek, Len Wein, and Kelley Jones*
ISBN 978-1-59307-648-1 | $17.99

**Conan and the Songs of the Dead**
*Joe R. Lansdale and Timothy Truman*
ISBN 978-1-59307-718-1 | $14.99

**Conan and the Midnight God**
*Josh Dysart, Will Conrad, and Jason Shawn Alexander*
ISBN 978-1-59307-852-2 | $14.99

**Conan: The Blood-Stained Crown and Other Stories**
*Kurt Busiek, Fabian Nicieza, Cary Nord, Eric Powell, Bruce Timm, and others*
ISBN 978-1-59307-886-7 | $14.99

# CONAN THE PHENOMENON
*Paul M. Sammon*
ISBN 978-1-59307-653-5 | $29.99

# KING CONAN
**Volume 1**
ISBN 978-1-59307-477-7 | $18.99

# CONAN ONGOING SERIES
**Volume 0: Born on the Battlefield**
TPB: ISBN 978-1-59307-981-9 | $17.99
HC: ISBN 978-1-59307-980-2 | $24.99

**Volume 1: The Frost Giant's Daughter and Other Stories**
*Kurt Busiek and Cary Nord*
ISBN 978-1-59307-301-5 | $15.99

**Volume 2: The God in the Bowl and Other Stories**
*Kurt Busiek and Cary Nord*
ISBN 978-1-59307-403-6 | $15.99

**Volume 3: The Tower of the Elephant and Other Stories**
*Kurt Busiek, Cary Nord, and Michael Wm. Kaluta*
ISBN 978-1-59307-547-7 | $15.99

**Volume 4: The Hall of the Dead and Other Stories**
*Kurt Busiek, Mike Mignola, Tim Truman, and Cary Nord*
ISBN 978-1-59307-775-4 | $17.99

**Volume 5: Rogues in the House and Other Stories**
*Timothy Truman, Cary Nord and Tomás Giorello*
ISBN 978-1-59307-903-1 | $17.99

**Volume 6: The Hand of Nergal**
*Timothy Truman and Tomás Giorello*
TPB: ISBN 978-1-59582-178-2 | $17.99
HC: ISBN 978-1-59582-179-9 | $24.99

**Volume 7: Cimmeria**
TPB: ISBN 978-1-59582-283-3 | $17.99
HC: ISBN 978-1-59582-341-0 | $24.99

**Volume 8: Black Colossus**
TPB: ISBN 978-1-59582-533-9 | $17.99
HC: ISBN 978-1-59582-507-0 | $24.99

**Volume 9: Free Companions**
ISBN 978-1-59582-592-6 | $17.99

# SAVAGE SWORD OF CONAN
*Roy Thomas, Barry Windsor-Smith, John Buscema, Alfredo Alcala, Pablo Marcos, and others*

**Volume 1**
ISBN 978-1-59307-838-6 | $17.99

**Volume 2**
ISBN 978-1-59307-894-2 | $17.99

**Volume 3**
ISBN 978-1-59307-960-4 | $19.99

**Volume 4**
ISBN 978-1-59582-149-2 | $19.99

**Volume 5**
ISBN 978-1-59582-175-1 | $19.99

**Volume 6**
ISBN 978-1-59582-375-5 | $19.99

**Volume 7**
ISBN 978-1-59582-510-0 | $19.99

**Volume 8**
ISBN 978-1-59582-582-7 | $19.99

# KULL

**KULL: THE SHADOW KINGDOM VOLUME 1**
Written by Arvid Nelson • Art by Will Conrad and José Villarrubia
ISBN 978-1-59582-385-4 | $18.99

**THE CHRONICLES OF KULL VOLUME 1: A KING COMES RIDING**
Written by Roy Thomas, Gerry Conway, and Len Wein •
Art by Wallace Wood, BernieWrightson, and others
ISBN 978-1-59582-413-4 | $18.99

**THE CHRONICLES OF KULL VOLUME 2:
THE HELL BENEATH ATLANTIS AND OTHER STORIES**
Written by Roy Thomas, Gerry Conway, and Len Wein • Art by Wallace Wood,
BernieWrightson, and others
ISBN 978-1-59582-413-4 | $18.99

**THE CHRONICLES OF KULL VOLUME 3:
SCREAMS IN THE DARK AND OTHER STORIES**
Written by Roy Thomas, Don Glut, and Steve Englehart •
Art by John Buscema, Ernie Chan, and Howard Chaykin
ISBN 978-1-59582-585-8 | $18.99

**KULL MINI-BUST: THE SAVAGE
SWORD COLLECTION #2**
$59.99